General editor: Graham Hand

Brodie's Notes on Willi

Henry IV Pa

A. J. P. Smith BA (Oxon)
English Department, Kingswood School, Bath

Pan Books London and Sydney

First published 1985 by Pan Books Ltd
Cavaye Place, London SW10 9PG
9 8 7 6 5 4 3 2

ISBN 0 330 50193 3
Photoset by Parker Typesetting Service, Leicester
Printed and bound in Great Britain by
Richard Clay (The Chaucer Press) Ltd, Bungay, Suffolk

Other titles by A. J. P. Smith in the Brodie's Notes series:
Richard II
Measure for Measure

Contents

Line references in these Notes are to the *Arden Shakespeare: Henry IV Part 1*, but as references are also given to particular acts and scenes, the Notes may be used with any edition of the play.

Preface

This student revision aid is based on the principle that in any close examination of Shakespeare's plays 'the text's the thing'. Seeing a performance, or listening to a tape or record of a performance, is essential and is in itself a valuable and stimulating experience in understanding and appreciation. However, a real evaluation of Shakespeare's greatness, of his universality and of the nature of his literary and dramatic art, can only be achieved by constant application to the texts of the plays themselves. These revised editions of Brodie's Notes are intended to supplement that process through detailed critical commentary.

The first aim of each book is to fix the whole play in the reader's mind by providing a concise summary of the plot, relating it back, where appropriate, to its source or sources. Subsequently the book provides a summary of each scene, followed by *critical comments*. These may convey its importance in the dramatic structure of the play, creation of atmosphere, indication of character development, significance of figurative language etc, and they will also explain or paraphrase difficult words or phrases and identify meaningful references. At the end of each act revision questions are set to test the student's specific and broad understanding and appreciation of the play.

An extended critical commentary follows this scene by scene analysis. This embraces such major elements as characterization, imagery, the use of blank verse and prose, soliloquies and other aspects of the play which the editor considers need close attention. The paramount aim is to send the reader back to the text. The book concludes with a series of revision questions which require a detailed knowledge of the play; the first of these has notes by the editor of what *might* be included in a written answer. The intention is to stimulate and to guide; the whole emphasis of this commentary is to encourage the student's *involvement* in the play, to develop disciplined critical responses and thus promote personal enrichment through the imaginative experience of our greatest writer.

Graham Handley

Shakespeare and the Elizabethan playhouse

William Shakespeare was born in Stratford-upon-Avon in 1564, and there are reasons to suppose that he came from a relatively prosperous family. He was probably educated at Stratford Grammar School and, at the age of eighteen, married Anne Hathaway, who was twenty-six. They had three children, a girl born shortly after their marriage, followed by twins in 1585 (the boy died in 1596). It seems likely that Shakespeare left for London shortly after a company of visiting players had visited Stratford in 1585, for by 1592 – according to the jealous testimony of one of his fellow-writers Robert Greene – he was certainly making his way both as actor and dramatist. The theatres were closed because of the plague in 1593; when they reopened Shakespeare worked with the Lord Chamberlain's men, later the King's men, and became a shareholder in each of the two theatres with which he was most closely associated, the Globe and the Blackfriars. He later purchased New Place, a considerable property in his home town of Stratford, to which he retired in 1611; there he entertained his great contemporary Ben Jonson (1572–1637) and the poet Michael Drayton (1563–1631). An astute businessman, Shakespeare lived comfortably in the town until his death in 1616.

This is a very brief outline of the life of our greatest writer, for little more can be said of him with certainty, though the plays – and poems – are living witness to the wisdom, humanity and many-faceted nature of the man. He was both popular and successful as a dramatist, perhaps less so as an actor. He probably began work as a dramatist in the late 1580s, by collaborating with other playwrights and adapting old plays, and by 1598 Francis Meres was paying tribute to his excellence in both comedy and tragedy. His first original play was probably *Love's Labour's Lost* (1590) and while the theatres were closed during the plague he wrote his narrative poems *Venus and Adonis* (1593) and *The Rape of Lucrece* (1594). The sonnets were almost certainly written in the 1590s, though not published until 1609; the first 126 are addressed to a young man who was his friend and patron, while the rest are concerned with the 'dark lady'.

The dating of Shakespeare's plays has exercised scholars ever since the publication of the First Folio (1623), which listed them as comedies, histories and tragedies. It seems more important to look at them chronologically as far as possible, in order to trace Shakespeare's considerable development as a dramatist. The first period, say to the middle of the 1590s, included such plays as *Love's Labour's Lost*, *The Comedy of Errors*, *Richard III*, *The Taming of the Shrew*, *Romeo and Juliet* and *Richard II*. These early plays embrace the categories listed in the First Folio, so that Shakespeare the craftsman is evident in his capacity for variety of subject and treatment. The next phase includes *A Midsummer's Night's Dream*, *The Merchant of Venice*, *Henry IV Parts 1 and 2*, *Henry V* and *Much Ado About Nothing*, as well as *Julius Caesar*, *As You Like It* and *Twelfth Night*. These are followed, in the early years of the century, by his great tragic period: *Hamlet*, *Othello*, *King Lear* and *Macbeth*, with *Antony and Cleopatra* and *Coriolanus* belonging to 1607–09. The final phase embraces the romances (1610–13), *Cymbeline*, *The Tempest* and *The Winter's Tale* and the historical play *Henry VIII*.

Each of these revision aids will place the individual text under examination in the chronology of the remarkable dramatic output that spanned twenty years from the early 1590s to about 1613. The practical theatre for which Shakespeare wrote and acted derived from the inn courtyards in which performances had taken place, the few playhouses in his day being modelled on their structure. They were circular or hexagonal in shape, allowing the balconies and boxes around the walls full view of the stage. This large stage, which had no scenery, jutted out into the pit, the most extensive part of the theatre, where the poorer people – the 'groundlings' – stood. There was no roof (though the Blackfriars, used from 1608 onwards, was an indoor theatre) and thus bad weather meant no performance. Certain plays were acted at court, and these private performances normally marked some special occasion. Costumes, often rich ones, were used, and music was a common feature, with musicians on or under the stage; this sometimes had additional features, for example a trapdoor to facilitate the entry of a ghost. Women were barred by law from appearing on stage, and all female parts were played by boy actors; this undoubtedly explains the many instances in Shakespeare where a woman has to conceal her identity by disguising

herself as a man, e.g. Rosalind in *As You Like It*, Viola in *Twelfth Night*.

Shakespeare and his contemporaries often adapted their plays from sources in history and literature, extending an incident or a myth or creating a dramatic narrative from known facts. They were always aware of their own audiences, and frequently included topical references, sometimes of a satirical flavour, which would appeal to – and be understood by – the groundlings as well as their wealthier patrons who occupied the boxes. Shakespeare obviously learned much from his fellow dramatists and actors, being on good terms with many of them. Ben Jonson paid generous tribute to him in the lines prefaced to the First Folio of Shakespeare's plays:

Thou art a monument without a tomb,
And art alive still, while thy book doth live
And we have wits to read, and praise to give.

Among his contemporaries were Thomas Kyd (1558–94) and Christopher Marlowe (1564–93). Kyd wrote *The Spanish Tragedy*, the revenge motif here foreshadowing the much more sophisticated treatment evident in *Hamlet*, while Marlowe evolved the 'mighty line' of blank verse, a combination of natural speech and elevated poetry. The quality and variety of Shakespeare's blank verse owes something to the innovatory brilliance of Marlowe, but carries the stamp of individuality, richness of association, technical virtuosity and, above all, the genius of imaginative power.

The texts of Shakespeare's plays are still rich sources for scholars, and the editors of these revision aids have used the Arden editions of Shakespeare, which are regarded as pre-eminent for their scholarly approach. They are strongly recommended for advanced students, but other editions, like The New Penguin Shakespeare, The New Swan, The Signet are all good annotated editions currently available. A reading list of selected reliable works on the play being studied is provided at the end of each commentary and students are advised to turn to these as their interest in the play deepens.

Literary terms used in these notes

Alliteration Occurs when several words of the same consonant sounds are juxtaposed.
Ambiguity Having two meanings.
Blank verse Verse which is of unrhymed iambic pentameters.
Catastrophe A climactic event which decides the outcome of a sequence of events.
Diction The way in which a writer chooses his words.
Dramatic irony Occurs when a character in a play speaks words the true significance of which he does not understand. The audience, however, is assumed to be in possession of the significance of the character's utterance.
Euphuism Over-elaborate use of language – highly artificial, stylized.
Imagery Figurative, rather than literal, language designed to enhance a reader's imaginative, sensory, intellectual response to what is being referred to. Often, more narrowly, applied to a work's similes and metaphors.
Irony Occurs when the surface meaning of a statement is at variance with its underlying meaning.
Metaphor A figure of speech in which a comparison is made between two (often dissimilar) things.
Onomatopoeia Occurs when the sound of a word or, words, matches the sense of what is being described.
Pathos The emotion of pity which may be aroused by a piece of writing.
Personification Occurs when an inanimate object is treated as though it were a person.
Pun A play on words that sound or are spelt the same but have very different meanings.
Simile A comparison introduced by 'like' or 'as'.
Soliloquy The name given to a character's speech when, alone on the stage, he speaks his inner thoughts directly to the audience.
Sub-plot That part of the story which is separate from the main sequence of the narrative.
Symbolism A sign or an emblem which stands for a concept by means of which a writer may arouse emotion in the reader.

The play
Plot, sources and treatment

Plot

Henry IV Part 1 continues the story of *Richard II*. Three of the Percy family, Thomas Earl of Worcester, his brother Henry, Earl of Northumberland, and the latter's son, nicknamed Hotspur, are stung by the ill-treatment meted out by Henry IV. He has made use of their services to depose Richard II and gain the throne for himself, and then has coolly cast them off. They therefore plan a rebellion against the King. The main plot of the play deals with the hatching of the conspiracy, leading up to the battle of Shrewsbury, in which Hotspur and Worcester, allied with a Scottish Earl, Douglas, are defeated by the King. Hotspur himself is slain by the Prince of Wales.

At the beginning of the play, the Prince spends most of his time with frequenters of taverns, and there are some lively scenes of low-life, the life and soul of which is a fat knight Sir John Falstaff. These scenes make the sub-plot (or comic plot). Thus the serious fight of the main plot is balanced by a comic fight in the sub-plot. Falstaff and others of the 'tavern-set' arrange a highway robbery of some rich travellers, but the Prince and one of his friends contrive in turn to rob them of their booty, for the sake of 'the incomprehensible lies that this same fat rogue will tell' about the odds against him in the encounter. Everything turns out as expected.

When the rebellion breaks out the Prince has to turn his mind to important things, and even Falstaff goes on active service and appears at the Battle of Shrewsbury.

As the play continues the story of *Richard II*, so it looks forward to *Henry IV, Part 2*. Although the King has won this battle, there are still other conspirators under arms, and the play ends with the King's plans to conquer them. These are put into effect in *Henry IV, Part 2*.

The historical period of the action of *Henry IV, Part 1* is nearly twelve months, between the Battle of Holmedon, 14 September 1402, and the Battle of Shrewsbury, 21 July 1403.

Sources and treatment

Shakespeare's main historical source when he came to write the play in about 1597, was Holinshed's *Chronicles of England, Scotland and Ireland* which had been published in 1577. This work interprets history from a Tudor standpoint and stresses the disastrous consequences for England of the deposition and murder of Richard II by Henry Bolingbroke. It also mentions the reformation of the Prince, but does not suggest any motivation – merely stating that he banished his 'misrulie mates' and forbade them to 'approach, lodge, or sojourne within ten miles of his court or presence'.

The origin for the low-life scenes would seem to be a play which had enjoyed some popularity, called *The Famous Victories of Henry V*. This crude work exploited the stories of Hal's youthful wildness, dramatizing in episodic fashion his riotous behaviour and loose-living friends – one of whom is named Jockey Oldcastle. In the early performance copies of *Henry IV Part 1*, Shakespeare retained the name Oldcastle for Hal's chief misleader, but on representations from the Oldcastle family, he changed the name in the first printed copy to Falstaff.

Samuel Daniel's *The First Fowre Bookes of the Ciuille Wars Between the Two Houses of Lancaster and Yorke* (1595) also seems to have influenced Shakespeare. In the third Book, Daniel deals with much the same material which appears in Holinshed, although he disagrees with him on some important points of detail – for example, Holinshed has Glendower fighting at Shrewsbury, whereas Daniel says that the Welsh were absent. Shakespeare obviously follows Daniel, adding the reason that Glendower was unable to come because he was 'o'er-ruled by prophecies'.

Another influence would seem to be the medieval Morality Plays which dealt with the age-old theme of the conflict between Vice and Virtue. In these plays Virtue was often depicted as a youthful Everyman, who was tempted by various manifestations of the Seven Deadly Sins, but eventually emerged triumphant. This bears an obvious similarity to the Prince's dealings with Falstaff.

In general terms Shakespeare relies upon Holinshed for the bare bones of history, but incorporates Daniel's version when it suits him dramatically. For example, he adopts Daniel's adjustment of chronology which makes Hotspur and Hal young, and the King old. Actually Hotspur was older than the King, who was thirty-seven at the time of the Battle of Shrewsbury. Hal was fifteen. Daniel and Shakespeare prefer to emphasize the rivalry between Hal and Hotspur. Shakespeare underlines (what is a suggestion in Daniel and a mere hint in Holinshed) that Hal overcame Hotspur.

From *Famous Victories*, as well as the Oldcastle/Falstaff character, Shakespeare derived Ned: an embryonic Poins. He also adapted from the same source, the Gad's Hill episode and the character Gadshill, but they are transformed almost beyond recognition. The goings-on in the tavern at Eastcheap in *Famous Victories* only serve to emphasize the superiority of Shakespeare's play.

Scene summaries, critical comment, textual notes and revision questions

Act I Scene 1

King Henry IV, who deposed Richard II, awaits the report from Westmoreland of the previous night's council meeting. High on the agenda had been the King's desire to launch a Crusade 'as far as the sepulchre of Christ', but trouble on the Welsh and Scottish borders has already forced the postponement of this undertaking for a year. From Westmoreland, the King receives no comfort: hoping for peace, he hears instead of a grievous defeat inflicted upon his forces by the Welsh irregulars under Glendower. Harry Percy, son of the Earl of Northumberland, has defeated the Scots at Holmedon but the young Percy (nick-named 'Hotspur') is refusing to behave according to the rules and hand over his prisoners: a blatant act of defiance to his king, which Westmoreland attributes to the malevolent and rebellious inspiration of Worcester. Nonetheless, the King ruefully envies Northumberland the prowess of Hotspur; his own Harry, heir to the throne which he usurped, only seems interested in leading a reprobate life amongst the dissolutes of London.

Commentary

The King's opening remarks express a desire for peace in his troubled realm; by the end of the scene it is apparent that this hope is to be frustrated. Of course, Henry came to the throne by means of usurpation, and we find invariably in Shakespeare that those who interfere with the divinely-appointed scheme of things do so at their peril. Thus, it should not surprise us that Henry is experiencing disturbance on many levels: he is ailing in body ('pale' and 'wan'); his kingdom is fraying at the edges (Wales and Scotland), and, even within his own family, his son refuses to behave in a prince-like manner, mixing freely with the riff-raff of London.

Henry had the reputation of being a schemer, who rarely did anything without there being an element of calculation. He determines to initiate a crusade in an effort to unite his kingdom in a common purpose. Also, we may suppose, it will enable him to atone for the sin which he committed in deposing the rightful king. Thus, in vain as it turns out, he hopes to kill two birds with one stone.

After he hears of the valiant deeds performed by Hotspur at Holmedon, the King laments the waywardness of his own son. A parallelism is thereby established between the two young men which has a far-reaching impact on our understanding of the play. Whilst Hotspur is enhancing his reputation on the battle-field, so that he may be described as the 'theme of honour's tongue', Hal is indulging in 'riot and dishonour'. Henry wishes to exchange sons with Northumberland. Much of the play is to be concerned with the redemption of Hal, who, by the end, is at one with his father. But Hotspur dies at Hal's hand, fighting in a rebel cause.

At the end of the scene Westmoreland seeks to establish Worcester as the villain of the piece by implying that he is encouraging Hotspur to defy the King. Hotspur, as we shall see, has many faults, but ruthless calculation is not one of them. This is a play of many parallels and contrasts: Worcester is Henry's counterpart in the rebel faction – nothing he does is without calculation, and it is understandable, therefore, that there is particular animosity between the two of them.

The poetry of the King's opening speech quickly establishes the mood of the play. We may note the prevalence of animal imagery, suggesting that England has become a country 'red in tooth and claw'. Peace is hunted and pants for breath.

we The King refers to himself and to his kingdom.

Find we . . . peace to pant The King urgently desires a breathing-space in order that he may divert minds intent on domestic disorder towards his projected Crusade.

breathe . . . of new broils Speak breathlessly about new wars.

stronds Shores.

thirsty entrance . . . own children's blood A powerful metaphor suggesting civil bloodshed, derived from Genesis, 4, 6 where the earth is described as opening its 'mouth' to receive the blood of Abel, after he had been slain by his brother, Cain.

trenching i.e. the earth is cut into trenches to channel away the blood of the slaughtered.

meteors . . . heaven The eyes of soldiers, which flash like meteors with the light of battle. Meteors were indications of divine displeasure and their appearance in the heavens were portents of earthly catatrophe.

All of one . . . substance bred Meteors were thought to be composed of vapour which was drawn up from the earth's atmosphere into the heavens. Thus domestic strife, like meteors, is pictured as sharing a common source. The combatants are all from the same country.

intestine Internal.
close Close-quarters.
mutual well-beseeming ranks Ranks which are united, as is befitting.
the sepulchre of Christ i.e. Jerusalem.
impressed Enlisted.
bootless Profitless.
Therefor . . . now That is not the purpose of this meeting.
hot in question Subject of urgent debate.
limits of the charge Limits to expenditure.
athwart Cutting across (our intention).
post Messenger.
Mortimer Edmund Mortimer, commander of the King's forces.
rude Barbaric.
corpse Corpses.
shameless transformation i.e. they mutilated the dead bodies.
match'd Put alongside.
uneven Rough, uncertain.
Holy-rood day September 14th.
sad Serious, sorrowful.
by Judging from.
shape of likelihood As it was likely to turn out.
true industrious friend Consistently and devotedly loyal.
variation of each soil i.e. Blunt is stained with the dirt of the many regions through which he travelled to reach London.
discomfited Routed.
Balk'd . . . blood Piled up in bloody ridges.
honourable spoil . . . gallant . . . prince i.e. Hotspur's 'princely' exploits are now immediately contrasted with the dishonourable conduct of the true prince.
the theme of honour's tongue i.e. Hotspur is the example of honour: whenever honour is mentioned he is often the subject of the conversation. It is also one of the main themes of the play, in, which Shakespeare examines the word and seeks to define it in terms of human conduct.
minion Darling.
him i.e. Hotspur.
Plantagenet Surname of the royal family at the time.
coz Kinsman.
surpris'd Captured.
aspects Respects.
prune Preen.
bristle up the crest This is a term derived from falconry, implying readiness.

Act I Scene 2

Our first meeting with the Prince seems to confirm his father's view of him. He keeps company with a fat knight, Sir John Falstaff, and the subject of their conversation is highway robbery, as well as the excessive eating and drinking in which Falstaff indulges. Poins enters with the news that pilgrims will be passing Gad's Hill in the early hours of the morning and that their fat purses will make them ideal victims. Falstaff is overjoyed at the thought of easy pickings, but Poins has a refinement to the plot in mind. Taking advantage of Falstaff's absence, Poins proposes to the Prince that they absent themselves from the actual robbery of the pilgrims and contrive to ambush Falstaff, depriving him of his ill-gotten gains at the very moment of his triumph. The glory of the jest will be to listen to the way in which Falstaff explains away the absence of the fruits of his endeavours. The Prince agrees to go along with Poins.

Alone for the first time, the Prince reveals that he is not the madcap reprobate that he pretends to be. He tells us that he mixes with the lower orders only temporarily. He intends to reform and when this reformation occurs, it will appear the more glorious because of its contrast with his unpromising present way of life.

Commentary

At once we can see that the King has reason to lament the conduct of his son, for he is consorting with a blatant rogue, whose main interests in life seem to be self-indulgence and highway robbery. There is much witty banter between Hal and Falstaff. But there is much more to Falstaff. For all his apparent age he has unquenchable vitality and resourcefulness. His roguishness is conducted with such verve and good humour that we are almost prepared to forgive him anything – as we shall see.

But we should not lose sight of what really is going on in this scene. Cut away the jests and it is clear that Hal is not the young man that Falstaff believes him to be. Hal's initial remarks to Falstaff reveal clearly that he understands the underlying wastefulness of Falstaff's life. Furthermore, many of the Prince's utterances have a cutting edge of realism about them: when Poins offers him a chance to rob some innocent travellers the Prince says that he will 'tarry at home'; Falstaff immediately denounces him as a 'traitor', to which the Prince coolly replies, 'I care not!' The Prince is only persuaded to join the scheme when Falstaff is the chosen victim. Here, and less obviously elsewhere, but consistently, the Prince distances himself from the excesses of the 'fat knight'. 'Do not thou, when thou art king, hang a thief,' says Falstaff. 'No,' replies Hal. 'thou shalt.' And, enigmatically, Falstaff is asked, 'Is not a buff jerkin a most sweet robe of durance?' Although he has no means of knowing it yet (unless there is something slightly uneasy about his harping on 'when thou art king'), Falstaff's days are numbered.

But what is the purpose behind the Prince's odd behaviour, which causes his father so much heartache? Things become clearer after the soliloquy which terminates the scene. Here Hal reveals that he is not really a 'madcap'; he will reform, and his present dissolute life will serve to heighten the appreciation of his reform when it does come. Thus his 'bad' behaviour may be seen as a calculated pose.

Shakespeare intends that we should draw some comparison between this scene and the previous one. First, we see that disorder in the nobility extends downwards to the lower echelons of society. In the one, robbers on a grand scale are plotting to rob a kingdom from a robber-king; in the other, petty thieves are planning to steal from the innocent.

The true royalty of the Prince is conveyed by the link implied between him and 'the sun'. He says that he intends, for example, to 'imitate the sun' and 'break through the foul and ugly mists'. The sun is a familiar symbol of royalty. Interestingly, and in contrast, Falstaff is associated with the moon ('we . . . go by the moon'; 'squires of the night'; 'Diana's foresters' etc.). Thus basic dissimilarities between Falstaff and Hal are emphasized. Fittingly, Falstaff takes as his patroness Diana: goddess of the moon and the hunt (linked with the highway robbing activities).

sack Falstaff's favourite tipple: a sweet, sherry-like white wine from Spain.
demand . . . know Ask what you really want to know. The implication is that the time of day is irrelevant to Falstaff, who measures time in terms of the succession of his various ungoverned appetites.
leaping-houses Brothels.
come near me now A pun. (1) You have come near the truth about me; (2) You are my near companion in these vices.
the seven stars The Pleiades.
Phoebus Greek sun-god.
'that wand'ring knight so fair' This is probably a reference to a popular ballad of Shakespeare's day.
sweet wag Dear boy.
Grace Falstaff enjoys a quibble on the possible meanings of this word: (1) as a term of address to a nobleman; (2) a blessing, before a meal; (3)

piety, being in a state of 'grace'. Falstaff's mocking self-correction is a way of taunting the Prince.

prologue to an egg and butter A reference to food eaten in Lent, and thus hardly worth saying grace for.

squires . . . beauty A difficult passage. The general sense seems to be that 'we who may be termed creatures of the night (thieves) must not ignore the beauty (booty) which may also be obtained by day. Note further puns on night/knight and body/bawdy.

Diana Roman goddess of chastity, the moon and hunting. The latter two attributes enable Falstaff to claim her as a patroness of his highway robbing activities.

as the sea is i.e. with regularity, like the tides.

countenance (1) the face (of the moon); (2) in a sense, Diana countenances (permits) their bad behaviour.

holds well Holds good.

for the fortune . . . gallows The Prince here shows himself adept at wittily re-interpreting Falstaff's remarks about their being 'minions of the moon' etc. The moon causes the tide to ebb and flow in just the same way that money acquired on one night is quickly spent the following morning. More ominously, the Prince goes on to remind Falstaff that the fortunes of men also ebb and flow like the tide; this applies especially to thieves, who, whether they realize it or not, are always in proximity to the gallows – either at the foot of the ladder, or, at their 'height', swinging from the gibbet itself. It is not surprising that Falstaff does not seek to prolong this line of wit.

Lay by The equivalent of 'Stand and deliver!'.

Bring in Supposedly spoken to an inn-keeper, telling him to 'bring in' more sack.

Hybla A town in Sicily, renowned for the excellence of its honey.

old lad of the castle The original Falstaff was called Sir John Oldcastle. Also a pun on 'The Castle', a notorious London brothel.

buff jerkin A leather jacket worn by the sheriff's men.

robe of durance Durable and associated with 'durance', meaning imprisonment. Again, a subject not close to Falstaff's heart.

quips . . . quiddities Witticisms . . . quibbles.

reckoning Another pun: Falstaff implies that he has called her to make up his bill and for sexual favours.

resolution . . . law Men of courage put off, as they are, by the deterrent of out-of-date laws.

Antic Buffoon.

brave Fine.

jumps . . . humour Suits my temperament.

court Punning on 'court' of justice and palace 'court'.

suits Punning on 'suits', this time meaning the clothes of the condemned man, which traditionally were appropriated by the hangman.

gib cat Tomcat.

lugged Bear-baiting involved the bear being tied by the neck to a stake and worried ('lugged') by dogs – a popular Elizabethan pastime.
hare Traditionally this is the most melancholy of animals. Its flesh was thought, when eaten, to produce nightmares and indigestion.
Moor-ditch A disgustingly filthly open drain, noted for its smell.
commodity Supply.
damnable iteration A devilish ability to quote the Bible.
thou hast . . . harm upon me Falstaff has the cheek to accuse the Prince of leading him astray. He then goes on to ask God to forgive Hal for this trespass. Typically Falstaff, in its pretended piety.
I'll be . . . Christendom Falstaff will not allow himself to be damned, even though a king's son may tempt him!
baffle Put me to shame.
set a match Set up a robbery.
merit i.e. good deeds.
cozening Cheating.
vizards Masks.
Yedward A familiar form of the name Edward.
chops Blubber-cheeks.
one i.e. one of the party.
want countenance Lack the approval (of people of influence and substance).
All-hallown summer Like the earlier remark 'latter spring', this refers to the fact that Falstaff's body is old, even though his spirit may be young. He's enjoying, in this sense, an 'Indian Summer'. Sunshine on 1 November – All Hallows Day!
wherein . . . to fail Where we need not turn up, if we so desire it.
habits Dress.
appointment Part of our equipment.
cases of buckram Suits of coarse cloth.
nonce Occasion.
noted Familiar.
doubt Fear, Hal is being sarcastic.
forswear Give up.
incomprehensible Boundless.
wards Guards (i.e. defensive moves, a term derived from fencing).
uphold Put up with.
unyok'd Unrestrained.
humour Mood, inclination.
accidents Events.
the debt I never promised i.e. the debt which it never seemed possible that he would pay.
sullen ground Dull background.
glitt'ring o'er Outshining. The 'fault' is compared to the 'sullen ground', the 'reformation' to the 'bright metal'.
foil Contrasting background.
to . . . skill To make profitable use of my misdeeds.

Redeeming time Making up for wasted time.

Act I Scene 3

In conference at Windsor Castle Henry IV confronts Worcester, Hotspur and Northumberland. The King opens proceedings by declaring that hitherto he has been too mild of manner; henceforth, rebellious subjects may expect a more authoritative approach. Worcester tactlessly remarks that the Percies do not look for such treatment, especially as they helped the King to gain the throne. Angrily, perceiving 'danger and disobedience' in Worcester's manner, the King dismisses him from the royal presence. Things now go from bad to worse. It becomes plain that Hotspur has no intention of meekly giving up his Scottish prisoners to the King. At first, Hotspur excuses his insubordination on the grounds that he was grossly offended by the King's effeminate messenger. Soon, however, it becomes apparent that the prisoners are to be a bargaining counter: the King may have them, provided that he pays the ransom for Mortimer, who is at present in the hands of Glendower. This is more than Henry can stomach, for he has heard that Mortimer betrayed him and ignominiously surrendered to the Welsh. To add insult to injury, the treacherous Mortimer has married Glendower's daughter, thus confirming his rebelliousness in the King's eyes. Hotspur vehemently defends Mortimer's honour, claiming that he fought very bravely in the battle on the banks of the Severn before he was captured. Henry storms from the council chamber, issuing threats and still demanding 'his' prisoners.

Worcester now returns, and, after some difficulty, manages to channel Hotspur's rage into the course that he has devised: outright rebellion. It is proposed that Hotspur will free the Scots and form an alliance with them against the King. Meanwhile, Worcester, who is confident that the Archbishop of York can easily be persuaded to join the rebel cause, will go to Wales and gather the support of Glendower and Mortimer. Thus a power will soon be raised of sufficient might to overthrow the ungrateful King.

Commentary

This scene begins with confrontation and ends in fragmentation. Both parties air their grievances: the King is still smarting under the insult implicit in Hotspur's denial of the Scottish prisoners, but this bone of contention merely highlights the underlying clash between him and the rebels. Worcester, Northumberland and Hotspur all feel slighted by Henry, whom they helped to the throne, and for whom they have no respect. The King feels threatened and wary of those who have already shown a tendency towards factionalism. Ironically, Henry is suffering for the disorder which he himself introduced into the realm by his revolt against the anointed Richard.

Henry begins by asserting that he is going to 'be myself' i.e. he is going to behave in a more blatantly regal fashion putting aside his more natural disposition, which he says 'hath been smooth as oil, soft as young down'. In other words, in order to be more kingly he is going to be less natural. Perhaps the father is as much an actor as the son?

Hotspur's energetic defence of his actions is typical in its vivid rendering. It was not a calculated insult, but occurred on the spur of the moment, but his continued refusal to go along with the King *is* calculated – and it's Worcester who does the calculating. Equally extravagant and tactless is Hotspur's defence of his brother-in-law Mortimer.

Henry and the Percies are clearly on a collision course and the scene ends with Worcester outlining a plot that has been carefully considered before this meeting took place. But it is also clear that there is a basic weakness in the rebel hierarchy. Worcester has the greatest difficulty in calming the incensed Hotspur, which bodes ill for the future of their plot. There are obvious temperamental differences between the two.

Hotspur also contrasts with Hal. In many ways, Hotspur is more obviously princely: he is renowned for his bravery on the field of battle, and, because of it, his honour is universally acknowledged. Yet here we see how vulnerable is such 'honour' – if it is naive, and lacks consideration and a moral dimension. Worcester easily manipulates it for an evil purpose. Hal's view of life is much more carefully thought out: tempted he may be, but he does not sell himself – not even to the winning ways of Falstaff. So long as his self-esteem remains intact, Hal evidently considers that his honour is intact: at this point in the play honour, for Hal, is a matter between himself and his conscience. For Hotspur, honour is a matter between himself and his public persona. His reputation is all-important: it cannot be shared with others, for that would diminish its currency in the world at large. Hence his antipathy to the ungrateful King and his contempt for the Prince, who consorts with the lower orders of society.

blood Temperament.
found me Found this out about me.
tread upon Treat contemptuously.
I . . . condition In future you may expect that I shall behave in a manner which befits my kingly status. You will find that I shall exert my might and inspire fear, rather than act according to my natural disposition.
title of Claim to.
Our house Our family (i.e. the Percies).
holp Helped.
portly Important. It is noteworthy that the Percies supported Henry in his bid for the throne, which culminated in the deposition of Richard II.
peremptory Arrogantly dogmatic.
moody Resentful.
servant brow This refers to the frowning brow which does not befit a king's subject.
deliver'd Reported.
envy Malice.
misprision Misunderstanding.
reap'd Close-clipped.
at harvest-home When the corn is cut and stacked.
milliner Seller of perfumed haberdashery.
pouncet-box Small box with perforations in the lid, through which perfumes may be sampled.
Took it in snuff I was angry.
holiday and lady Affected and effeminate.
popinjay Parrot.
grief Pain.
God save the mark! God save us from evil!
sovereignest Finest.
parmacity Spermaceti (a fatty substance derived from the sperm whale).
saltpetre An ingredient of gunpowder.
tall Brave.
bald unjointed Trivial disconnected.
indirectly Without attention.
for As.
die i.e. be forgotten.
so . . . it now So long as he declares now that he did not mean what he said on that previous occasion.
Earl of March Mortimer (though historically he did not hold this title).
buy Reward.
indent with fears Strike a bargain with those whom we fear.

revolted Rebellious.
fall off Given way to disloyalty, fail in his duty.
But . . . of war Except in so far as he suffered a misfortune of war.
one tongue . . . wounds His many wounds speak on his behalf.
mouthed Gaping like open mouths.
confound Spend.
changing hardiment Exchanging blows, or engaged in a violent combat of varying fortunes.
breath'd Paused to catch their breaths.
crisp Rippled, or curly-headed.
bare Threadbare, or possibly barefaced.
policy Scheming, plotting.
colour Disguise, cover up.
so many This refers to 'wounds'.
belie Misrepresent.
kind Manner.
license Permit.
make a hazard Risk losing.
'Zounds By God's wounds!
on his part On his behalf.
ingrate and canker'd Ungrateful and corrupt.
Bolingbroke Henry IV was Henry Bolingbroke before he usurped Richard II.
hear Fit of passion.
eye of death This could refer to a look which threatened death to Hotspur, but more probably it suggests that the King's eyes were filled with mortal fear.
in us From us.
intercepted Interrupted.
the world's wide mouth According to public report.
wear . . . murderous subornation Bear the dishonourable reputation of secret murderers.
base second means Inferior secondary agents.
the line Level, limit or rope.
predicament Category.
you range You may be classified.
gage Pledge ('nobility and power').
unjust behalf An unjust cause i.e. Bolingbroke's.
canker Dog-rose, which grows wild, as distinct from the cultivated variety, hence 'corrupted' here.
disdain'd Degraded.
quick-conceiving discontents i.e. minds made quick to understand by reason of the discontents which they feel.
adventurous spirit The spirit of daring. Notice how Worcester tailors his appeal to the character of Hotspur.
unsteadfast footing of a spear An allusion to a commonplace of medieval romance in which a knight was required to cross a raging torrent with no more secure a'bridge' than a spear or sword. Again,

specifically designed to appeal to Hotspur, who could never resist a perilous challenge.

good night . . . swim In any case he will be finished.

So honour cross it Provided that honour crosses its path.

grapple Come to a fight. Dangers, from wherever they arrive, are welcome so long as they can be met in honourable battle.

corrival Partner, competitor.

half-fac'd Shared. Hotspur cannot tolerate that honour should be shared; to him this would be half-hearted. If there is any honour to be won, he wants it all for himself.

figures Language, images.

form Substance.

audience A hearing.

Scot A pun: (1) Scotsman; (2) a payment of little value.

start away Are going off the point.

studies Purposes.

gall and pinch Annoy and torment.

sword-and-buckler A buckler (small shield) together with a sword was commonly worn by the lower orders. This is a contemptuous reference to the low, swaggering company which the Prince keeps.

pot of ale Again, a reference to the low tastes of the Prince.

Tying . . . thine own Listening to no other voice than your own.

pismires Ants.

politician Schemer – always used pejoratively by Shakespeare.

kept Lived.

candy deal Sugary amount.

fawning Cringing, in a flattering manner. Dogs are frequently associated by Shakespeare with insincere affection.

Look when Whenever.

cozeners Cheaters.

stay Await.

mean for powers Means for raising soldiers.

divers Various.

prelate High-ranking man of the Church.

bears hard Bears a grudge (because of . . .).

Bristow Bristol.

in estimation Guessingly.

ruminated Carefully thought out.

that occasion . . . bring it on The opportunity to bring it about.

game . . . let'st slip . . . Metaphor from letting loose greyhounds after their prey, implying hastiness before the plan is put into action.

aim'd Directed.

a head An army (an obvious pun in this line).

even Correctly.

home Back.

No further go . . . your course Worcester is anxious to keep control of Hotspur, whose rashness might ruin his carefully devised plot.

suddenly Shortly.
steal A word which obviously implies stealth: Worcester condemns himself by the words he chooses.
powers Armies.
To bear . . . arms To take their own fates in their hands and put things to the test in battle.
at With.
fields Battlefields.
sport A characteristic view of battle.

Revision questions on Act I

1 What do we learn of the political situation in England from the first act?
2 From the evidence of Scene 2, do you feel that the King's anxieties about his son are justified?
3 Find points of comparison and contrast between Hostpur and Hal.
4 Discuss the part played by Worcester in Act I.
5 Compare and contrast the 'high life' scenes with the 'low life' scene in Act I.

Act II Scene 1

We meet two carriers, who are preparing to set out for Charing Cross from an inn-yard at Rochester. The presence of Gadshill indicates that they are shortly to encounter the highway robbers. The carriers are wary and are unwilling to divulge any information to Gadshill – not even the hour; they certainly won't let him get his hands on their lantern! A chamberlain, also in league with the robbers, arrives and there follows some entertaining verbal by-play with Gadshill.

Commentary

This scene presents a glimpse of common folk going about their business in a down-to-earth setting. On one level, its function is to provide comic relief – a 'rest' for an audience which has just experienced the high emotion of the previous scene. The vernacular of the carriers is a welcome relief after Hotspur's flights of metaphorical fancy and the cool strains of Worcester's cynical scheming.

However, there are some relevant parallels between this scene and those which have preceded it: here we meet petty criminals, but we have already met major criminals amongst the nobility, who are plotting to seize a kingdom. Indeed, the King himself came by the throne illegally. The 'management' of both inn and country is bad, and both are, in a sense, 'verminous'. The disorder and suspicion in this scene are reflections in miniature of undesirable elements which are apparent in society as a whole. In both 'worlds' there is a suggestion that the dishonest thrive, at least for the moment.

four . . . day Four o'clock in the morning.
Charles' wain The Great Bear or Plough.
yet Still.
ostler Stableman, groom.
Anon At once.
Cut The name of the horse.
few flocks in the point i.e. to provide some padding over the pommel (point) of the saddle.
jade A broken-down old horse.
wrung in the withers Sore across the shoulder-blades.
out of all cess Beyond all measure.
Peas and beans The staple diet of horses.
dank Damp.
next Surest.
bots Worms.
never joyed Had no pleasure from life.
tench A fish which was thought to be particularly subject to parasites.
christen Christian.
jordan Chamber-pot.
leak . . . chimney Urinate in the fireplace.
chamber-lye Urine.
loach Species of fish.
razes Bundles of roots.
pannier Saddle-bag.
pate Head.
faith Trustworthiness.
know . . . two No one pulls a fast one on me.
Lend . . . lantern He thinks that Gadshill may steal his lantern!
Time . . . candle He is being deliberately vague.
with company In a group.
have great charge Are carrying merchandise of great value.
'At hand . . . pick-purse' Another popular saying: 'Always close at hand, said the pickpocket.'
even . . . chamberlain As good as saying, 'At hand, said the chamberlain.' A disparaging remark which implies that most chamberlains are pickpockets.
variest no more Are no more at variance with.
latest . . . how Set up robberies.

current Good.
franklin A small landowner.
Wild Weald.
three hundred marks A large sum of money.
auditor An officer of the Exchequer.
abundance of charge Much to be in charge of.
presently Immediately.
Saint Nicholas' The patron saint of highwaymen (his 'clerks' or scholars).
Troyans 'Trojans' – fine fellows. Refers, of course, to the presence of the Prince and Poins.
to do . . . grace Bring honour to the profession (of thieving).
make all whole Put things right again (if things misfire).
foot-landrakers Robbers who go about on foot, 'raking in' whatever they can get.
long-staff sixpenny strikers Thieves who strike a man down with a staff for a mere sixpence.
mad . . . maltworms Crazed, purple-faced, moustached drunkards.
burgomasters Town dignitaries.
onyers An obscure word. Some take it to mean 'great ones', others believe it to mean 'accountants'.
hold in Stand their ground, or able to keep a confidence.
boots Yet another pun, this time the quibble is upon 'boots' and 'booty'.
hold . . . way Keep the water out on a muddy road, i.e. 'will she protect you if you get into trouble?'
justice . . . her The law-enforcers have been bribed, just like a pair of water-proof boots have been 'greased'. Perhaps, too, there is a suggestion that the judges are drunk (as well as being available to be bribed).
receipt Recipe.
fern-seed Supposed to make invisible those who carried it.
purchase Spoils.
'homo' (Lat.). Gadshill means that they are all men, irrespective of whether they are true or false, implying that there is not much to choose between them.

Act II Scene 2

The robbery at Gad's Hill. From the outset, Falstaff finds that things do not quite go according to plan: his horse has been 'removed' and he does not relish having to carry his own weight around. Also, he finds that at the critical moment, he has to confront his victims without the help of the Prince and Poins. Nonetheless, the travellers are relieved of their possessions. Falstaff accuses the Prince of 'arrant' cowardice. The ultimate disaster then happens, and Falstaff is himself robbed by two mysterious strangers. He does not put up much of a fight to defend his recently-acquired booty.

The jest, at Falstaff's expense, has worked; he has not recognized his assailants, who gleefully contemplate their triumph – and Falstaff's ignominy.

Commentary

This scene is full of fun – most of it at Falstaff's expense. Much is made of his huge bulk and consequent lack of mobility. Of course, it is robbery of the innocent nonetheless, and it is committed on the King's highway. Shakespeare does not involve the Prince in the actual deed of theft; thus he is distanced from overt villainy. It is 'permissible', however, that he should rob Falstaff and later in the play we learn that the victims are to be reimbursed.

It is characteristic of Falstaff that he should pretend to be young: in reality, he is old and his moral decadence is related to his physical decline. Yet, in another sense, Falstaff is young: his body houses a lively spirit. Hence the ambiguity of our feelings about him, which Shakespeare intends. An old man who finds that his inner self is still youthful has its tragic aspect and equally, it may have its comic side, as evidenced in this scene. Falstaff is the 'Lord of Misrule' and related to the character of Vice in the old morality plays. He represents reversed values and is clearly opposed to good order; in this scene, we may notice his predeliction for accusing others of his own weaknesses (cowardice, for example) and his consistent presentation of the Prince as *his* corrupter!

The robbery gives plenty of opportunity for stage 'business' and the spectacle of the robbers robbed in hilarious. Clearly, Shakespeare intends that we should not dwell too much on the nature of the crime – all is subsumed in a welter of action and high spirits. The misfortune of the travellers is almost incidental, the main stress falling unreservedly on the discomforting of Falstaff.

gummed velvet Gum was used to stiffen velvet.
close Hidden.
squier Foot-rule.
break my wind Be out of breath.
I doubt . . . all this Falstaff expects to enjoy a happy after-life on account of all this suffering which he is at present having to endure.
forsworn Sworn to give up.

medicines Drugs.
starve Die.
true Honest.
veriest varlet Greatest rogue.
afoot On foot.
colt Fool.
heir-apparent garters A popular tag: 'He may hang himself in his own garters' is here linked with the fact that, as heir to the throne, the Prince would be a Knight of the Garter.
peach Give you away by turning king's evidence.
ballads And having betrayed them to the law, Falstaff will see to it that their crimes against him will be ridiculed in a ballad, possibly to be sold to celebrate their execution.
is so forward Exceeds the limits.
setter Informant.
Case ye Disguise yourselves.
Gaunt Falstaff plays upon the sound here of 'Paunch' and 'Gaunt'. John of Gaunt, the Prince's grandfather, is said to have been very thin.
happy . . . dole Proverbial. 'May each one's fortune be to be a happy man.'
caterpillars Voracious feeders (on the good in society).
youth Falstaff frequently like to think of himself as young, despite physical evidence to the contrary.
gorbellied Pot-bellied.
chuffs Wealthy misers.
jure Make jurors of you (irony).
Now . . . and I Now if you and I could . . .
argument Topic of conversation.
share Divide the proceeds.
arrant Out-and-out.
no equity stirring No justice in the world.
lean earth Implies that even the round globe of the whole earth is lean by the side of Falstaff.

Act II Scene 3

Hotspur reads a letter. The sender is anonymous and is about to back out from the plot to overthrow the King, Hotspur impatiently despises such faint-heartedness, which he thinks stems from cowardice. There is some fear, however, that this waverer will betray their purposes to the King. Incidentally, we learn that the conspirators are due to meet 'by the ninth of the next month'.

Kate (Hotspur's wife), a loving and lively young woman, asks why her husband's demeanour towards her has changed so much of late. He has become sullen, quarrelsome, his sleep has been disturbed and he appears uncharacteristically indifferent towards her. Hotspur's replies are evasive and non-committal. Kate must perforce accept his immediate departure on secret business which he will not divulge to her. She will follow him tomorrow.

Commentary

From the standpoint of the rebels, there are some ominous signs in this scene. It seems, that even before the enterprise gets underway, they are about to lose a supporter, and the fault, it is implied, is Hotspur's, The anonymous letter-writter is a person who should not have been asked for his support in the first place – Hotspur has revealed too much and to the wrong person.

It is evident that Hotspur has been having doubts about the wisdom of the plot, although he dare not express these worries even to himself, preferring to cheer himself up by reeling off a list of those who support him. But Kate's picture of her husband's behaviour during the past fortnight reveals a deeply troubled spirit. To Shakespeare, disturbance of sleep is commonly a symptom of guilt and fear. Also, we are shown how the strain of public events is adversely affecting Hotspur's private life. There are now secrets between husband and wife; ironically, the scene began by indicating Hostpur's inability to keep secrets.

In his relationship with his wife, Hotspur reveals that he has a softer side to his nature. He clearly loves Kate and in his own bluff manner expresses his affection for her. Kate responds by twisting his little finger, in the hope that by this means she may persuade him to reveal what is troubling him! She fails, but the incident has charm and a sort of tenderness. Here we may notice a contrast with the Prince, for unlike Hal, Hotspur is unable to reconcile the private and the public aspects of his life: hence the sad estrangement from the woman he deeply loves. Hal, on the other hand, although he appears divided between the world of the King and that of Falstaff, in reality is perfectly clear-headed about what he wants from life and how he intends to achieve it. Hotspur, an essentially divided man, dissipates his great energies; whereas Hal, an apparently divided man, single-minded pursues his goal: to be an effective King, when the time comes.

house Family.
take Catch.

counterpoise . . . opposition So great a weight is set on the opposite side of the scale against you.
hind Peasant.
very sincerity of fear Heavy sarcasm. Hotspur foresees that he will go and tell all to the King out of fearfulness for the success of the venture, whilst pretending to be a good and loyal subject.
bend Turn.
thick-eyed Dull-eyed.
curst Bad-tempered.
manage Giving orders to.
sallies, and retires The to and fro of battle.
palisadoes Defence-works.
frontiers Ramparts.
basilisks, culverin Types of cannon.
currents Changing fortunes.
heady Headstrong.
motions Expressions.
hest Command.
heavy Serious.
back Climb on his back.
Esperance The family motto: 'Hope'.
spleen Irritability.
title i.e. claim to the throne.
line Support.
paraquito Parrot.
mammets Dolls.
crowns . . . current A pun on 'crowns' meaning 'heads' and 'coins'. Cracked crowns (coins) would not normally pass as legal currency, but in these times cracked crowns (heads) are to be very much prized.
reason whereabout Ask for what reason.
closer More discreet.
of force Of necessity.

Act II Scene 4

The scene opens in the tavern, where we find the Prince and Poins awaiting the return of Falstaff, who arrives before long. He and his henchmen appear to have been involved in a fight; they are covered in blood. To explain the lack of spoils from the robbery, Falstaff unfolds a tale of how he was set upon by numerous assailants, and how, after putting up tremendous resistance against overwhelming (and ever-increasing) odds, he was forced to surrender his recently-won prize. All this is larded with frequent references to the cowardice of Hal and Poins, who deserted their friend in his hour of need. In the course of this fabrication, Falstaff lets slip that the attackers were wearing

Kendal green. The Prince decides to put a halt to the lies by asking Falstaff how he could see colours if it was pitch dark. Momentarily disconcerted, Falstaff plays for time and refuses to give a reason 'under compulsion'. But it is time for the bubble to be burst and the Prince confronts the 'heroic' Sir John with his abject cowardice: 'We two set on you four . . .' How will Falstaff explain this away? Scarcely pausing for breath, Falstaff avers that he knew that it was the Prince who was attacking him, and clearly it would not be right for the heir-apparent to be killed. Instinctively, Falstaff claims that he perceived the true identity of the Prince, and consequently gave up the fight: 'I was now a coward on instinct.'

Fortunately for the fat knight, the Hostess announces the sudden arrival of a nobleman from the court and Falstaff exits to send him packing. From Peto and Bardolph, Hal learns the shameful truth of the Falstaffian subterfuge.

Sir John returns with the news that a rebellion is imminent and the Prince has been summoned to a meeting with his father. Perhaps seeking to disconcert Hal, Falstaff taunts him with the fearsome reputations of the rebel leaders and the anger that he is likely to encounter from the King. Hal seems unmoved but agrees to act out an improvised play as a rehearsal for what may be an awkward scene with his father. Falstaff will play the King, Hal will be himself. In the 'drama' which follows, Falstaff eagerly flatters himself at the expense of blackening the characters of everyone else. But then the roles are reversed: Falstaff will play the Prince and Hal will be the King.

Now Falstaff finds himself on the receiving end and must listen to an unrelenting appraisal of his character. There is an awkward hiatus after Hal has asserted that ultimately he will 'banish plump Jack', which is interrupted by the arrival of constables and a sheriff, who have followed a hue and cry to the tavern. Before he can be apprehended, Falstaff is concealed behind an arras, where he promptly falls into a drunken slumber.

Hal defends Falstaff by equivocally telling the sheriff that the 'gross fat man' is 'not here', but promises to make him answer any charges which may be laid.

Finally, the Prince and Poins pick the pocket of the somnolent Falstaff. They are amazed, at finding a bill which reveals much expenditure on sack accompanied by the minimum outlay on bread. In business-like tones, the Prince reminds the company that they must 'all to these wars'; Falstaff will be given charge of a company of foot-soldiers. The stolen money will be paid back, with interest. Falstaff sleeps on.

Commentary

The Prince may have been with the lower classes but he is clearly not one of them. He has been an observer and the statement, 'when I am King of England I shall command all the good lads of Eastcheap!' points to the reason for this excursion below-stairs. As Henry V, Hal will put to good use the knowledge that he has gained: he will be able to identify with their needs and anxieties. Furthermore, it will serve to remind him of his common bond with humanity.

The Prince's evocation of the home life of Hotspur is a brilliant parody of the Hotspur we already know. Hal is relaxed enough about his rival to be able to satirize his reputation, but Hotspur is not denigrated – there is respect in the portrait.

Falstaff's entry with his motley crew is one of the comic highlights of the play. Falstaff is no scheming villain; he lives for the moment and this sense of spontaneity is nowhere more apparent than in this scene. There is an inspirational quality about him. If there is a 'starting-hole' into which he may bolt, at the last minute, he will find it. However, by certain references linking him with the 'Vice' character in the Morality Plays, Shakespeare 'places' Falstaff, morally speaking. And taken overall, one of the main themes of this scene is the unmasking of Falstaff.

The moment of truth arrives at the end of the extemporized play. It had begun as a joke: an ideal opportunity for Falstaff to play the virtuous, much put-upon, old (but young!) man. The joke becomes serious when Hal plays the King. We become aware that, in fact, this is no longer playing, but 'real'. For a moment, we glimpse the future when Hal will be King and his first act will be to don the mantle of royalty and reject Falstaff. Acting the part of his father, Hal bombards the old knight with a catalogue of his follies which must perforce penetrate and wound. Falstaff affects not to understand and defends himself, but to no avail. The telling episode ends on the note of banishment and the frightening silence is broken, significanty, by the obtrusive knocking of law and order. At this moment neither the Prince nor Falstaff is acting.

It is left to the Prince, almost off-handedly, to defend his erstwhile colleague from the rigours of the law– he can afford to do so, because he can be confident in himself, that whatever hold

Falstaff may have had upon him, has departed. Besides, there are more important matters concerning the state to be taken in hand. Without fuss, the Prince accepts his duty to go to his father and to go 'to the wars'. Meanwhile, Falstaff sleeps on, oblivious and 'out of the picture'.

It will be noticed that this scene has brought together the comic sub-plot and the political plot of the play. Here for the first time Hal talks of Hotspur – his political and moral rival. A nobleman from the court recalls Hal to his father. Towards the end there are many reminders of the war which looms on the horizon. And, of course, the mock-play presents us with a comic miniature of court life and the misrule which threatens the kingdom.

fat room Room containing wine-vats.
hogsheads Blockheads.
I . . . humility I have humbled myself to the very depths. A metaphor from a stringed musical instrument. 'Base'=bass.
leash Trio; normally applied to three hounds leashed together.
drawers Waiters.
take it . . . salvation Will lay their salvation on it.
courtesy Good manners.
Jack Fellow.
Corinthian An accepted companion.
good boy i.e. one of the boys.
dyeing scarlet A slang expression, presumably derived from the scarlet complexion which a hard-drinking man acquires.
breathe . . . watering Pause for breath, whilst drinking.
play it off Swig it down.
tinker Tinkers were renowned for their drinking ability, and possessed their own colloquial language.
honour This speech began with 'humility' and ends with 'honour'. Significantly the Prince's honour has been gained from an unlikely source: his willingness to encounter even the most humble.
underskinker Under-waiter.
Score Put 'on the slate', allow him credit.
bastard Spanish wine.
Half-moon Name given to one of the rooms at the inn.
never leave Don't stop.
precedent Example.
Pomgarnet The name of another room: 'Pomegranate'.
serve i.e. of his apprenticeship.
By'r Lady An oath: 'By Our Lady'.
lease Term.
books Bibles.
Michaelmas 29th September.

Anon, anon Jestingly, the Prince pretends to understand that Francis has demanded immediate payment of a thousand pounds.
leathern-jerkin, crystal-button Leather jacket with crystal buttons. The items in this list make up the traditional clothing and appurtenances of a vintner.
not-pated Close-cropped.
agate-ring A ring with a seal carved in the agate.
puke-stocking Stockings of a dark-grey, or blue-black, woollen material ('puke').
caddis-garter Worsted ribbon used for garters.
Spanish pouch A leather pouch of the Spanish fashion.
Why then . . . to so much Deliberate gibberish, designed to confuse the hapless Francis.
cunning match Clever devices. Poins is not appreciative of the Prince's joke; he expected something more.
issue Outcome, result.
I am now . . . at midnight I am now in the mood to enjoy any kind of fancy that exists or has ever existed. i.e. 'I'm ready for absolutely anything that comes along.'
That ever Who would believe that.
his industry . . . reckoning His work consists solely of running up and downstairs and all he can talk about is adding up bills.
I am not yet . . . mind Hal says that he is not yet ready to be of a similar mind to Percy. The implication is that the time is not far away when he will be as familiar with the foibles of Hotspur as he has just shown himself to be with those of Francis.
drench Dose of medicine.
brawn Fat boar.
Rivo! A drinking cry.
Ribs . . .Tallow Hal refers to Falstaff as if he were a rib of beef or a lump of suet.
nether-stocks Stockings.
foot them Wear them on my feet.
Titan . . . of the sun's Titan is the sun-god (Hyperion). The reference here likens Falstaff supping his sack to the effect of the sun on a dish of butter. Both sack and butter melt away!
compound Combination i.e. Falstaff's red face over the glass of sack. (Like the red sun over the butter dish).
lime i.e. it's been 'doctored'. Lime was added to sack to improve its appearance but a connoisseur cannot be fooled.
shotten herring i.e. a herring that has spawned and thus is thin and useless.
God help the while! God help these times!
weaver Falstaff is adopting the role of a Puritan. Weavers were often Calvinist refugees who had fled from Flanders because of religious persecution. They were pious and used to sing psalms whilst working. Note that, once again, Falstaff is pretending to be virtuous.

If I do not . . . lath A dagger of wood was a stage prop of the character 'Vice' in the morality plays. Critics have made much of this remark, suggesting that Shakespeare is hinting to the audience a way of estimating the moral worth of Falstaff.
whoreson Bastard.
backing of your friends A pun upon 'showing your back to' i.e. running away, and 'supporting'.
All . . . that It doesn't matter.
half-sword At close-quarters.
buckler Small round shield.
ecce signum 'Behold the sign' i.e. the evidence.
dealt Fought.
Ebrew Jew 'A Jew of Jews'.
bunch of radish A reference which suggests thinness.
paid Put paid to them, killed them.
horse Fool.
ward Style of fencing.
I . . . point This is how I defended myself and how I pointed my sword.
mainly With might and main.
target Falstaff's small shield has now become a large battle-shield!
points . . . hose Poins puns on two meanings of 'points': the tip of a sword and the laces which held up a person's breeches.
clay-brained Dull, stupid.
knotty-pated Block-headed.
tallow-catch A pan used to catch the fat which dropped from roasting meat, or a form of 'tallow-keech' fat which was used to make candles.
strappado A form of torture. The victim was raised and lowered from the ground by means of his wrists which were tied behind his back.
sanguine Red-faced.
eel-skin Of barely any thickness. Sometimes emended to 'elf-skin'.
neat's tongue Ox tongue.
bull's pizzle Bull's penis.
stock-fish Fish which was cut into thin strips to be dried in the sun.
tailor's-yard i.e. yard measure.
bow-case A long, thin case in which bows were kept.
vile standing tuck Repulsive, upward-pointing rapier.
out-faced Frightened.
starting-hole Bolt-hole, into which you might escape.
Hercules Hero of Roman mythology, famed for heroism and feats of strength.
The lion . . . true prince It was popularly believed that lions would not attack anyone of royal blood.
on Because of.
clap Shut.
argument Subject.
a royal An Elizabethan coin. Hal jests: 'If a man has come with a

'noble' (another coin), then give him a 'royal' (a coin of greater value) to go away again!'

Swear truth out of England Swear to such a degree that truth itself would have to quit the country.

with the manner Caught red-handed.

extempore Uncontrollably.

fire i.e. your fiery features.

meteors, exhalations Shining, fiery objects in the sky (portents of disaster). A reference to the red pimples on Bardolph's face – enough to put the fear of God into anyone.

Hot livers . . . purses Implying drunkenness and consequent poverty.

Choler Anger. Hal goes on to pun on 'collar'/'halter' (hangman's noose).

bombast Material used for stuffing cushions and high-flown language.

Amamon A demon.

bastinado A torture involving beating the soles of the victim's feet.

made Lucifer cuckold Had the audacity to commit adultery with Lucifer's wife. Give the Devil his horns.

cross of a Welsh hook Glendower made the Devil swear to be his liegeman on the cross of a Welsh pikestaff.

mettle Spirit.

run A pun. Douglas is of such a fine mettle (metal) that he will never run (melt) away.

cuckoo i.e. have only one cry. Falstaff wishes that the Prince would drop this particular topic, i.e. 'running away'.

blue-caps Scots.

buy maidenheads . . . by the hundreds The point behind this remark is that because of the onset of civil strife what was previously held to be of great value may now be obtained very cheaply. The bottom has dropped out of the market. Here, in particular, virgins will not regard it as worthwhile to hang on to their virginity – they may be dead before long (or raped).

thrill Shiver.

whit Jot.

chid Rebuked.

state Chair of state.

joint-stool Stool made by a joiner.

and If.

King Cambyses' vein A reference to a play on the life of Cambises, King of Persia. It was written in a flowery, ranting style, which Falstaff proposes to emulate in his playing of King Henry.

leg Offered as part of an elaborate bow.

holds . . . countenance Keeps a straight face. The Hostess, referred to as the Queen (a pun on queen=prostitute), admires Falstaff's acting technique. The assembled riff-raff are the 'nobility' of Falstaff's court.

tristful Queen The Hostess is crying with laughter.

harlotry players Rascally actors.

tickle-brain Dealer in strong drink.
camomile An aromatic herb.
partly . . . partly An insulting imputation about the legitimacy of Hal.
pointed at i.e. held up to public scorn.
sun of heaven A significant pun. A verbal echo with Hal's own intention to behave like the sun in his soliloquy which ends I, 2.
micher Truant.
eat blackberries The idea is that Hal is like a naughty boy who prefers to play truant from school and go blackberrying.
virtuous man Falstaff himself, of course. Again he reverses the reality of the situation.
corpulent Well-built.
carriage Bearing.
lewdly given Inclined towards evil-doing.
peremptorily Without fear of contradiction.
rabbit-sucker A suckling rabbit.
poulter's hare Like the rabbit a trivial animal; here, a hare hung up for sale in a poulterer's shop.
set Seated.
tickled ye for a young prince Make you laugh with my impersonation of a young prince.
carried . . . from grace Out of my royal favour.
tun Hogshead.
trunk of humours Body full of foul fluids (humours).
bolting-hutch A bin in which impurities were collected when flour was sifted.
parcel of dropsies Container of superfluous bodily liquids.
bombard A large leathern drinking vessel.
cloak-bag Valise, for carrying clothes.
Manningtree ox An Essex town which annually roasted a whole ox, also famous for its morality plays. Hal in his remarks to Falstaff uses many terms connected with Morality Plays: 'vice', 'iniquity', 'ruffian', 'vanity' – all corrupting influences in the drama.
reverend . . . in years The adjectives here all stress the inappropriateness of Falstaff's conduct. He is an old man who should behave like one, and he is old enough to know better.
neat Clean.
cleanly Skilful.
cunning Talented.
craft Deceitfulness.
take me with you Let me know what you mean.
But . . . know Is Falstaff still playing the Prince, or is he speaking for himself?
Pharoah's lean kine See Genesis, 41, 19–21.
monstrous watch Large number of watchmen.
devil . . . fiddlestick Proverbial. 'Stop making mountains out of molehills!'

essentially . . . seeming so You are a person of true worth, even if you don't seem to be so (and, by implication, so am I).
major Major proposition.
cart i.e. a hangman's cart.
halter Hangman's noose.
arras Wall-curtain.
date Time is up.
The man . . . not here Obviously, the Prince's reply is ambiguous.
oily Slippery.
Paul's i.e. St Paul's Cathedral.
ob. A ha'penny.
deal Quantity.
a charge of foot A company of foot-soldiers.
his death . . . score He'll be dead after marching twelve score paces.
advantage Interest.
betimes Early.

Revision questions on Act II

1 Outline the story of the highway robbery from the Carriers' point of view.
2 From your reading of Act II what do you deduce about everyday life in England at the time of the play?
3 What do you find of significance to the play as a whole in Act II Scene 2?
4 Show how Falstaff exercises his nimble wits in Act II.
5 What impression of Prince Hal are you given by the scene in the tavern?

Act III Scene 1

The rebels meet, under the auspices of Glendower, to discuss how the country should be divided up after the war, and to put the finishing touches to their plans. Mortimer is hopeful of a successful outcome to the campaign, but Hotspur has forgotten the vital map. Glendower retrieves the situation, produces a map, and business is resumed. There is an immediate clash of temperaments: Glendower is wildly superstitious, arrogant and fanciful; Hotspur finds him tediously ludicrous. They quarrel. Mortimer acts as peacemaker and business is resumed. Another conflict arises: Hotspur disputes the boundaries which have been drawn on the map. The winding Trent deprives him of a particularly valuable piece of land: he will alter the course of the river to make things more equitable. There is another clash. In order to preserve the alliance, Glendower gives way: Hotspur may have the Trent dammed. Hotspur then says that he was bargaining only for the sake of bargaining, and now that he has got his way, he will be magnanimous – the Trent can flow its natural course! Agreement is reached.

Glendower departs and Mortimer rebukes Hotspur for baiting his father-in-law. Hotspur expresses contempt for Glendower's bombast and his superstitious nature. Worcester also rebukes Hotspur for his lack of tact, at which Hotspur professes himself 'schooled'.

Glendower returns with the wives of Mortimer and Hotspur. Unfortunately, the Welsh Lady cannot speak a word of English: this is very frustrating for Mortimer, but she sings charmingly and her tears testify to her sorrow at the imminent departure of her husband. Hotspur enjoys some banter with Kate, who is far too genteel (according to Hotspur) in her manner of oath-swearing. She refuses to sing.

It only remains for seals to be attached to the documents. All depart on a note of urgency.

Commentary

Shakespeare's audience would have regarded the prospect of a divided kingdom with the utmost horror. The Wars of the Roses, and the possibility of civil strife after the death of Elizabeth I, haunted the imagination of Englishmen at the close of the 16th century. Thus what is being discussed for much of this scene should be properly regarded as an abomination: antithetical to all who believe in good government, order and the will of the Almighty for his people on earth.

Hotspur's forgetting of the map does not bode well for the future of the campaign, which must depend on the efficiency of its leadership. Doubtless, this lapse was caused by Hotspur's eagerness for action. Glendower is revealed as a fanciful dreamer, living in a world of the occult, but he is practical enough to realize that he must concede to Hotspur in the interests of obtaining harmony in the rebel camp. It is typical that Hostpur, having won the point and satisfied his craving for honour, should then give way. This gesture, to his way of thinking, would heighten his reputation still further; in fact, it has the effect of exasperating Glendower beyond measure. Hotspur's honour demands that he brooks no rival, hence his desire to humiliate the proud Welshman. Ironically, Hotspur shares

Glendower's propensity for living in a world of make-believe.

The mood of dissension is softened towards the end of the scene, partly through the efforts of Worcester and Mortimer, but mainly by the arrival of the ladies. There is a contrast here, as well as a similarity. Both couples are clearly in love, but Mortimer's affection for his wife is expressed in terms of misty romanticism, frustrated by the language barrier. The song enhances the mood of melancholy, which the lovers feel because of their parting, and Glendower, acting as interpreter for his daughter, finds his poeticism well-suited to the task. Hotspur's love for Kate finds expression in terms of gentle teasing. In a sense, he too finds Kate's language frustrating – she should learn to swear properly, he cannot comprehend how a wife of his can use such milk-and-water oaths. He has no time for the striking of attitudes, and his manner with his wife is down-to-earth. It earns from Kate a dogmatic 'I will not sing.'

the parties sure Our people are reliable.
induction Beginning.
the front of heaven Simply, 'the heavens'.
cressets Torches.
frame Framework.
teeming Fruitful.
enlargement Release.
beldam, grandam Grandmother.
distemperature Disorder.
passion Suffering, pain.
courses Ways, happenings.
clipp'd in Surrounded by.
chides Rubs against.
read Taught.
Can trace me Who can follow me.
art Magic.
holds me . . . experiments Keep up with me when it comes to magical practices.
made head . . . power Opposed my forces.
Bootless Empty-handed. Hotspur seizes the opportunity for the obvious pun in his reply.
weather-beaten Glendower believes that he has control over the elements.
agues Fevers.
right What we have a right to. In fact, they have a right to nothing.
threefold order ta'en According to the respective 'rights' of the three of them.
limits Regions.
hitherto To this place.

indentures tripartite Three-way agreements.
interchangeably i.e. each indenture bearing the seals of all three of them.
execute Finalize.
father Father-in-law.
in my conduct In my safe keeping.
moiety Share.
cranking Winding.
monstrous cantle Huge slice.
indent Curve.
So rich a bottom So fertile a valley.
advantage Disadvantage.
Gelding . . . continent Cutting out from the opposite bank.
charge Expenditure.
cape Jutting-out portion.
in Welsh i.e. so that nobody will be able to understand you.
framed to Set to music of.
brazen canstick turn'd The sound of a brass candlestick being burnished, giving rise to a hideous scraping sound.
wheel . . . axle-tree Wheels and axles were made of wood. They squeaked if they had not been lubricated.
gait Walking.
cavil . . . hair Find reasons to raise objections over the most trivial matter.
Break with Break the news to.
moldwarp Mole.
Merlin . . . prophecies Magician and prophet of Welsh folk-lore. There was an ancient prophecy that the kingdom of the mole (Henry IV) would be divided up by a dragon, a lion and a wolf. These beasts were to be found on the family crests of the Glendowers, Mortimers and the Percies. Hotspur discounts all this mumbo-jumbo.
clip-wing'd Short-winged.
couching, rampant Heraldic terms. 'Lying down' (with head raised), 'rearing'.
skimble-skamble Meaningless.
'hum', 'Well, go to!' Symptomatic of utter boredom.
cates Delicacies.
profited . . . concealments Expert in occult matters.
temper Temperament, character.
natural scope Normal tendencies.
'cross his humour Into conflict with his inclinations.
wilful-blame To blame for letting your feelings run away with you.
blood Spirit, bravery.
dearest grace Noblest attribute.
opinion High-handedness.
men's hearts i.e. their approval.
beguiling . . . commendation Robbing them of their reputation.

spite Misfortune.
aunt Here, and throughout the play, Shakespeare muddles two Edmund Mortimers. It matters not, but historically the Mortimer in question was Lady Percy's brother.
peevish Fretful, wayward foolishness.
That pretty Welsh i.e. her tears are eloquent.
I . . . perfect in I understand only too well.
such a parley Such language, i.e. tears.
a feeling disputation A conversation of feelings.
ditties highly-penn'd Elaborate love-songs.
bow'r Boudoir.
division Musical variation.
melt Dissolve into tears.
wanton Luxuriant.
crown Give sway to.
heaviness Drowsiness.
heavenly-harness'd team The team of horses which pulls the chariot of the sun-god across the heavens.
our book Our accord, treaty.
those musicians The fanciful Glendower tells the couple that they will hear music from supernatural musicians.
straight Straightaway.
brach Bitch (refers usually to a hound).
comfit-maker's wife Confectioner's wife.
sarcenet Thin silk i.e. insubstantial.
Finsbury A very respectable area of London in the Elizabethan period.
pepper-gingerbread . . . guards A light confection which crumbled in the mouth, favoured by the bourgeois whilst out for a walk wearing their best clothing (with all the velvet trimmings).
Sunday citizens i.e. wearing their Sunday Best.
turn tailor Turning into tailor and start singing at your work.
redbreast teacher Singing teacher to robins.
seal Put our seals to the documents.

Act III Scene 2

At last, the Prince and his father come face to face. The King's first thought is that the dissolute behaviour of his son must be God's way of exacting retribution for his past sins. Hal replies, not unreasonably, that the King should not believe all the rumours which he has heard, but he admits that there is truth in some of the stories of his indiscretions. For these follies, the Prince asks for his father's pardon. Henry is not satisfied and specifically charges Hal with absenting himself from the deliberations of state and the low-life company which he has been keeping – such behaviour is totally inappropriate for a Prince. Henry reminds Hal of the dangers of flirting with popularity amongst the masses. This was the folly of Richard II, who led a life given over to trivialities and surrounded himself with fools. In the end, Richard was an object of blatant scorn and mockery. The policy of the King (Bolingbroke as he then was) involved holding himself aloof, so that when he did show himself, he was the more admired and sought after. Unable to maintain his composure, Henry breaks down and weeps at the estrangement between himself and his son.

The Prince vows that henceforth he will 'be more himself'. Henry cannot avoid drawing a parallel between past and present. When he landed at Ravenspurgh he enjoyed a fame similar to that which is now given to Hotspur. The concomitant of this is that Hal is like King Richard. The conclusion is inevitable: Hotspur is more fitted to be heir to the throne of England than Hal – his powers of leadership and battle honours prove it. Henry's final speculation is that his own son is so 'degenerate' that he will probably join the rebel faction.

The Prince's reply is direct and forceful. He will destroy Hotspur, and in so doing, will take possession of all his rival's honours. Thus he will prove himself a true son of the King and it will be clear that Percy, without realizing it, has merely been a 'factor', employed to garner up honours to hand them over to his conqueror, when the time comes. This vow the Prince will keep, or die in the attempt. The King is convinced of his son's loyalty and worth. Hal is given a position of trust in the King's army.

Blunt enters with the news that the rebels have met at Shrewsbury, a fact of which Henry had already been apprised. The Prince is directed to make his march through Gloucestershire and meet his father at Bridgnorth.

Commentary

Henry confronts the Prince as a king and as a father. As King he unflinchingly catalogues his grievances against Hal; as a father, he weeps. We are given some insight into the King during this scene. It is plain that Henry is burdened by the guilt which he feels on account of his usurpation of the throne. The tenor of much of what he says bears witness to the deep-seated malaise which threatens to overwhelm him: Hal must be a punishment from Heaven; implicitly, it must have been right to overthrow such a worthless king. Henry harks back to the past, and reveals the shrewd way in which he gained popularity and made his triumphant return from exile. Yet seeking to be strong, the fact is that he presides over a divided kingdom, and this scene, as did the first scene, reminds us that he is sick at heart.

But help comes from an unexpected quarter: the son will be the father's 'salve'. Equal to his father in subtlety, but adopting an entirely different approach, the Prince shows that he will be the support his father needs, now that the hour of trial has come. The King, as Bolingbroke, had indulged in the machinations of rebellion and usurpation; his son, much more fruitfully as it turns out, indulged a taste for the tavern life of Eastcheap. The King has not been able to shake off the burden of his 'mistreadings', but as we have just seen, Hal has wrestled with the devil and emerged victorious. The parallels and contrasts between father and son are many. Both believe in holding themselves aloof: but Hal aloof from the court, his father aloof from the masses. Both make a dramatic appearance on the political scene from a position of exile: but Hal's exile is self-induced, whereas his father was banished. Henry is a king who tries to come to terms with being a man; Hal is a young man who is coming to terms with being a future king. The problems of being 'human' and a king defeated Richard. Henry suppresses, fairly successfully for most of the time, his guilt and his anxieties about the future – but he never finally frees himself from his burdens. Hal, however, has investigated his shared humanity with the lowest in the kingdom, and the self-knowledge which he has gained will help him to come to terms with, if not to solve, the duality involved in being a king.

There remains the question of Hotspur. The King's final accusations against Hal have the effect of focusing our attention on the forthcoming 'trial of honour' between the two young men. During the scene, several general issues have been raised: we have ranged over the past and reached some resolution of the issues which faced father and son about the present. The scene ends by looking towards the future. The previous scene ended on a similar note; the conflict is imminent. The difference between the two parties, however, is most striking. The Glendower scene was full of underlying discord, which was never really resolved. Also, we remember from an earlier scene that supporters are growing cold about the rebellion. In contrast, Henry is moving from a position of weakness to a position of strength. This scene, above all others so far, illustrates the knitting together of the King's realm.

secret doom Hidden book of judgement.
blood i.e. heirs.
revengement Revenge.
inordinate Unworthy.
attempts Exploits.
match'd withal Linked with.
hold their level Equate themselves with.
Quit Acquit.
clear Blameless.
doubtless Certain.
ear of greatness i.e. must come to the ears of the King.
pickthanks Flatterers.
base Malicious.
true submission By submitting myself truly to you.
affections Inclinations.
hold a wing Keep their course. A falconry term.
forethink Anticipate.
common-hackney'd Cheaply familiar.
kept . . . possession Would have loyalty to the possessor. i.e. Richard II.
reputeless nameless.
stole all courtesy from heaven I seemed to be graced with courtesy from heaven.
state State appearances.
solemnity Respect.
skipping Prancing.
bavin A bundle of brushwood with which a fire was kindled.
carded Debased his royal stature.
gave . . . his name Allowed his royalty to become diminished. By his desire to be seen he allowed the crown to become too commonly available.
gibing Mocking.
stand the push Put up with the insolence.
comparative Dealers in insults.
Enfeoff'd Gave.
surfeited Overfull with.
cuckoo in June i.e. superfluous.
community Familiarity.
extraordinary i.e. the people looked upon the king as nothing out of the ordinary.
slept . . . face i.e. did not bother to wake up in his presence.
aspect Look.
cloudy Sullen.
participation Companionship.
more . . . the state Worthier to be called king.
the shadow of succession Your barely existent right to the succession.
colour Pretence.

Turns head Turns his forces towards.
in debt to years than Older than.
hot incursions Fierce inroads.
chief majority Pre-eminence.
capital Foremost.
discomfited Defeated.
ta'en Captured.
Enlarged Set him free.
To fill . . . defiance up To make a louder roar of defiance.
Capitulate Have raised an army.
up Up in arms.
vassal Slavish.
Base inclination Low inclinations of your character.
start of spleen The prompting of bad temper.
dog Lick the boots of.
favours Features.
whene'er it lights Whenever it arrives.
factor Agent.
engross Accumulate.
render Surrender.
worship of his time Honour acquired during his lifetime.
reckoning Account.
salve Heal.
parcel Part.
charge Command.
advertisement News.
business valued Estimated what we have to do.
Advantage . . . delay Whilst we delay we give great advantage to our enemies.

Act III Scene 3

The tavern in Eastcheap. Falstaff is sure that he is losing weight. Bardolph does not seem convinced and has to endure a series of insulting comments on his 'colourful' countenance. There is some talk of approaching death and Falstaff thinks it might be a good time to start going to church again. The Hostess enters and is immediately accused of keeping a disorderly house: after all, Falstaff has just discovered that somebody has picked his pocket. In reply, the Hostess demands repayment of the considerable debt which Falstaff owes her. She is next on the receiving end of a number of insulting comments about her sexual habits.

The mention of the Prince's name provokes Falstaff into saying that if he were here he would 'cudgel' him – at which moment Hal enters. More insults are flung at the Hostess, who manages to avert the flow by reminding Falstaff of his intention to 'cudgel' Hal. Cornered by the Prince's polite inquiry if this is true, Falstaff falls back on his old defence: how could he be expected to do harm to a king's son? This time he does not actually mention 'instinct'. Hal berates Falstaff for his dishonesty in accusing the poor Hostess and informs 'the embossed rascal' that he knows the contents of his pockets, and they contained no item of value, contrary to Falstaff's earlier claims. Cornered again, Falstaff misapplies Scripture as a defence, and demands that the Prince 'confess' to the villainy of pocket-picking. Falstaff eventually pronounces himself 'pacified'.

The scene ends with the Prince telling Falstaff that the stolen money from the highway robbery has been paid back, and that he has procured him command over a company of infantry. The Prince exits, issuing orders for the morrow. Falstaff is left alone on stage, calling for his breakfast and lamenting that the tavern cannot be the place from which he might conduct his recruiting campaign.

Commentary

Falstaff's opening remarks about his loss of weight are not meant seriously, he is referring probably to the effect of the strenuous activity he indulged in at Gad's Hill. But in an important sense they are true. Falstaff has dwindled in the sense that his influence over the Prince, which was always more imagined than real, has waned, and the evidence was plain at the end of the previous tavern scene. The talk of death and hellfire also suggests that all is not well with Falstaff; we begin to sense the beginning of his end. These motifs mirror, too, the decline of the forces of disaster in the political sphere.

Falstaff is described as 'fretful', and his mocking of Bardolph, whilst admittedly funny, is not very edifying. The stress of what is said by the Hostess is all on the theme of 'paying back' and in her way, this ignorant but good-hearted woman, is an unrelenting judge of Falstaff's less agreeable side. Again, despite the comedy, we feel that Falstaff is being called to account.

It is easy enough for the old, fat knight to hold his own with the foolish and stupid, but the Prince is a different matter. Once again, Falstaff's need to be ashamed is emphasized. Hal has little time now for Falstaff's excuses and 'escapes' – he is peremptorily given charge of a company of infantry and left on his own to contemplate the prospect of war.

fallen away Grown thin.
Action i.e. the robbery.
bate Lose weight.
apple-john Apple with a wrinkled skin.
in some liking In the mood for it.
peppercorn A ludicrous comparison: a peppercorn is very small, but it *is* dry and shrivelled!
in good compass In moderation.
admiral Flagship.
Knight of the Burning Lamp 'The Knight of the Burning Sword' – a well-known figure of chivalric romance.
death's-head A skull, a reminder of mortality.
memento mori Reminder of death.
Dives See Luke 15, 19–31, the parable of Dives and Lazarus.
God's angel Angels were supposed to appear in fire. Falstaff is fond of Scripture.
given over i.e. to the devil.
ignis fatuus Will o' the wisp.
ball of wildfire Firework.
purchase Purchasing power.
triumph Spectacle.
links Torches, flares.
salamander Lizard supposed to live in fire.
Partlet the hen Traditional name for a hen, or a busybody woman.
tithe The tenth part.
beguile Cheat.
Dowlas A strong coarse linen.
bolters Sieving cloths.
holland Fine linen.
ell Forty-five inches.
by-drinkings Drinks between meals.
rich Alludes to the 'rich' colours in Bardolph's face.
denier The tenth part of a penny.
younker A young man, still inexperienced.
Jack Rogue.
sneak-up Sneaky rascal.
is . . . door 'Is that the way the wind blows?'
stewed prune 'Stews'=a synonym for brothel, hence 'prostitute'.
drawn fox i.e. drawn from its den, and attempting to return to safety.
Maid Marian A female familiar in May Day celebrations. A character who had come to be regarded as disreputable.
a deputy . . . to thee i.e. compared with you, Maid Marian would be considered a highly respectable woman.
to have her A sexual innuendo.
embossed rascal A pun. Swollen or foaming at the mouth (of a deer). 'Rascal' is a name given to a lean young deer.
injuries i.e. so-called injuries.

tractable Amenable, willing.
pacified still Always disposed to make peace.
answered Cleared up.
with unwashed hands Right now (before you've even had time to wash your hands).
charge of foot Command of foot-soldiers
steal i.e. a horse-thief.
they offend . . . virtuous Rebels are offensive to virtuous men, they offend Falstaff, therefore Falstaff must be virtuous. Falstaffian logic!
Temple Hall Probably one of the Inns of Court.
furniture Equipment.
I could . . . drum 'If only this tavern were the recruiting depot' i.e. where the sound of the recruiting drum could be heard.

Revision questions on Act III

1 Describe how Hotspur nearly wrecks the rebels' council-meeting.
2 Outline the rebels' plan of battle against the King.
3 What is the effect of the interlude with the ladies at the end of Scene 1?
4 Outline the King's grievances against his son.
5 Do you find anything less attractive about Falstaff in Scene 3, as compared with his earlier appearances in the play? Quote evidence.

Act IV Scene 1

At Shrewsbury, the conspirators discuss the approaching battle. Hotspur and the Earl of Douglas exchange compliments. They are interrupted by a messenger who brings them the news that Northumberland is sick and unable to lead his army into the field. Hotspur does not share Worcester's opinion that Northumberland's absence is a 'maim' to them, rather he sees it as an insurance should things go wrong. If they lose the battle then Northumberland and his forces will enable them to make a come-back. Douglas agrees with this opinion, but Worcester remains doubtful, believing that many will think that Northumberland is deliberately holding back – thus raising a question-mark over the entire enterprise. Hotspur prefers to believe that Northumberland's absence lends a 'larger dare' to the cause and will indicate to onlookers that the rebels must be confident of success.

Sir Richard Vernon arrives to tell them that the Prince of

Wales, together with John of Lancaster, the Earl of Westmoreland and the King himself are preparing to meet the rebel forces at the head of a mighty army. Hotspur makes some dismissive remarks about the Prince but Sir Richard's description of Hal 'gallantly armed' does not tally with Hotspur's expectation.

More bad news arrives: Glendower is unable to come and will require a fortnight to assemble his army. Facing fearsome odds, Hotspur utters his call to battle: 'Doomsday is near; die all, die merrily.'

Commentary

There is much brave talk in this scene but it cannot disguise that the rebels' position is becoming increasingly precarious. As the imagery of Hotspur and Douglas indicates, what formerly seemed secure has now become a reckless gamble. We see the rebel forces dwindling before our eyes, just as it was apparent that Falstaff had dwindled in the previous scene. Only Worcester maintains a grasp of reality.

Impressions of sickness and decline abound: we are told that Northumberland is literally ill; the rebel army, says Worcester, has suffered a 'maim'; the eulogy of the Prince 'doth nourish agues'. In brief, Hotspur is right when he perceives that 'the very lifeblood' of their enterprise seems infected by an 'inward sickness'. Also, as in the previous scene, Death makes its presence felt: it figures six times in the last four lines.

In contrast, Vernon's eulogy of the Prince is full of health and vigour: he and his comrades are like refreshed eagles; they are 'as full of spirit as the month of May'; they are as exuberant as 'youthful goats'. The passage is sprinkled with the traditional symbols of royalty: gold, the sun, eagles. At the centre of this glittering array we find the Prince: he vaults into his saddle with the grace of an angel; his strength controls a 'fiery Pegasus'. Hal is portrayed as the epitome of chivalry. The references to his shining, glittering, sun-like appearance remind us of the promise he made at the end of Act I Scene 2, Hal has emerged triumphantly from behind dark clouds, his wildness not subdued, but now its energy controlled and channelled in an honourable direction.

attribution Recognition, praise.
season's stamp Minting of these times.

so general . . . world Should be so generally accepted. The metaphor comes from minting coins. The Douglas has a widely current reputation for valour – as bright and widely-accepted as freshly-minted coins.
soothers Flatterers.
task me Put to the test.
approve Try.
beard Confront him in arms.
justling Unsettled.
government Command.
bear Reveal.
fear'd i.e. they feared for his life.
whole Healthy.
deputation Deputy.
drawn Assembled.
remov'd Less involved.
advertisement Advice.
conjunction Combination of forces.
possess'd Informed.
main Handicap.
present want Absence at this time.
Seems . . . find it Appears worse than it will be in reality.
exact . . . cast Stake our entire fortune on one throw of the dice.
nice Precarious, risky.
maim Army or a stake in gambling.
hazard Chance, or the name of a gambling game.
very list Extremity.
bound Boundary.
sweet reversion A hope of future success, inheritance.
comfort of retirement Insurance to fall back on.
quality and hair Character and nature.
apprehension Perception.
fearful faction Timid conspiracy.
off'ring Challenging.
strict arbitrement Too cautious assessment.
sight-holes Holes through which observation may be made prior to shooting.
draws Opens.
strain too far Take things too far.
lustre Polish, shine.
dare Daring.
make a head Raise an army.
intended Is about to set forth.
daft Cast aside.
furnish'd Equipped.
estridges Ostriches. Ostrich plumes are the emblem of the Prince of Wales.

Bated Shook their wings.
coats Coats of armour, or coats of arms.
like images i.e. decked for a festival.
Wanton Sprightly.
beaver Helmet.
cushes Thigh-pieces (armour).
Mercury Roman messenger of the gods, usually represented wearing winged sandals, hence 'winged'.
wind Wheel around. Pegasus was the winged horse of Greek mythology.
witch Bewitch.
the sun in March Thought to be a particularly dangerous time for catching diseases, when the sun would draw up noxious vapours from the wet ground, and thus cause infection.
agues Fevers.
in their trim Decked out ready for sacrifice.
maid of smoky war Bellona, goddess of war.
reprisal Prize.
taste Put my horse to the test.
this Before (a fortnight).
serve Be sufficient.
die . . . merrily If die we must, let us die smiling.
out of i.e. have no (fear).

Act IV Scene 2

Still prepared to cadge from Bardolph, Falstaff has nonetheless struck it rich. Ordered to raise a company of men to fight for the King, he first conscripts men who have money and least wish to fight. He then permits them to buy themselves out and fills their places with the underdogs and misfits of society. Proud of his methods, he boasts of having made 'three hundred and odd pounds'. The only embarrassment is that he has to lead around a company of 'scarecrows'.

The Prince is not impressed with the quality of Sir John's fighting-men. Falstaff callously replies that they will do as well as the next man when it comes to being killed.

Commentary

Chivalry belongs to Prince Hal and Hotspur; the darker side of war is the province of Falstaff. His methods of recruitment are despicable and his attitude towards the pitiful specimens who form his 'charge of foot' is deplorable. It would be going too far to suggest that he is no longer an enjoyable character, but our laughter is tempered by our revulsion at his callous exploitation of those who are least able to take care of themselves. We must beware of seeing this scene solely through twentieth-century eyes: war, for Shakespeare, is not in itself an evil. Nonetheless, he appreciates its brutalities and Falstaff is one example amongst many of those 'who did well out of the war'.

Sutton Co'fil' Sutton Coldfield. Clearly, Falstaff has strayed from the direct route to Shrewsbury.
Lay out Pay for it from your own pocket.
angel Coin.
take it Falstaff deliberately misunderstands the meaning of 'makes'.
answer the coinage Undertake to guarantee it genuine.
soused gurnet A pickled fish.
press A royal warrant which endorsed compulsory military service.
of For.
householders, yeomen's sons i.e. men with sufficient resources to buy themselves out of the army.
contracted Engaged.
commodity Collection. Falstaff treats the men as though they were commodities, to be bought and sold.
warm slaves Subjects (of the King) who were passionately in love.
drum i.e. summoning them to the colours.
caliver Musket.
struck Hit and wounded by a bullet.
fowl Wild-fowl.
toasts-and-butter Self-indulgent people, who could enjoy the luxury of toast and butter. 'Milk-sops'.
bought . . . services i.e. bribed Falstaff to release them from military service.
ancients Those carrying the standards.
gentlemen of companies Lesser officers.
Lazarus See Luke 16, 19–31.
painted cloth Cheap, imitation tapestry.
discarded Dismissed.
unjust Dishonest.
younger . . . brothers Particular unfortunates who were deprived of inheritance of the family wealth.
revolted Runaway.
trade-fallen Unemployed owing to bad times.
cankers Parasites, who grow fat in time of peace.
fazed ancient Tattered flag.
rooms Places.
prodigals Another Biblical reference. See Luke 15, 16.
draff Pig-swill.

gibbets Roadside gallows.
gyves Fetters.
linen . . . hedge It was the practice to hang washing out to dry on the hedgerows, thus making it easy to steal.
blown A pun. Blown up like a balloon and out of breath.
quilt Padded leather jacket.
looks for Expects.
toss i.e. on the end of a pikestaff.
food for powder i.e. cannon-fodder.
pit Mass grave.
three fingers i.e. three fingers' thickness of fat.

Act IV Scene 3

Hotspur is for launching an immediate attack on the King's forces. Vernon and Worcester counsel caution: the rebel forces are wearied and not yet properly assembled. Sir Walter Blunt brings an offer of pardon from the King, together with a promise that Henry will listen to their grievances and seek to redress any wrongs. Hotspur, recounting the devious means whereby the King came to the throne, is not disposed to trust him on this occasion. After outlining Henry's recent treatment of Mortimer, Worcester, Northumberland and himself, Hotspur changes tack and asks that he be allowed the night to think over the King's proposal. So long as he is granted a safe-conduct, Worcester will deliver the answer in person on the morrow.

Commentary

The snappy exchange between Hotspur, Vernon and Worcester betrays the nervousness of the rebels as they face the King's army on the night before battle. The intervention of Blunt allows Shakespeare to review the shaky manner in which Henry came to the throne. Hotspur's reply recalls the King's deviousness, his readiness to make use of his supporters and the moral fudging of the issues involved in usurpation. Henry's behaviour does not justify the rebellion: it explains it. The inevitable consequence of killing the rightful king, and disturbing the true line of succession, is plain for all to see: disaffected friends, a kingdom threatened with chaos and on the brink of civil war.

supply Reinforcement.
well-respected Well-considered.

journey-bated Exhausted by their journey.
vouchsafe Grant.
our determination Our persuasion.
quality Party.
defend Forbid.
out of limit Beyond the bounds of good order.
charge Duty.
conjure Summon up (often used in the sense of conjuring up evil spirits).
suggestion Promptings.
Sick Weak, despised.
unminded Disregarded.
To sue his livery Claim what was rightly his after his father's death.
zeal Loyalty.
more and less The high and the low.
with cap and knee Bare-headed and kneeling (as a mark of respect).
in lanes Rank upon rank.
golden multitudes Richly-dressed crowds.
as greatness knows itself As he became aware of his own greatness.
Steps . . . higher Climbs a little higher.
blood Spirit.
strait Strict.
Cries out upon Denounces publicly.
seeming . . . justice Appearance of being just.
In deputation As deputies.
in the neck of Immediately following.
task'd Taxed.
if . . . well-placed If everybody owned what rightfully belonged to him.
engag'd Held hostage.
Disgrac'd Slighted.
intelligence Spies.
rated Chided.
head of safety Army of self-protection.
withal Moreover.
indirect Corrupt, not in direct line of succession.
impawn'd Pledged.
surety Guarantee.

Act IV Scene 4

The Archbishop of York, one of the supporters of the rebellion, is despatching letters arranging for those of the confederates who are left to 'make strong against the King', assuming that he wins the battle at Shrewsbury.

Commentary

This scene provides a short pause before the events which are about to take place at Shrewsbury.

The imminent defeat of the rebels is anticipated: the King is strong, they are weak. The Archbishop's remarks look forward to the aftermath of the battle, when it will be necessary for the rebellious faction to lick their wounds and perhaps fight again. Shakespeare thus looks forward to the events which are to be chronicled in *Henry IV Part 2*.

Hie Hurry.
brief Document.
lord marshal Thomas Mowbray. Later he became a rebel.
tenor General meaning.
bide the touch Be put to the test.
in the first proportion Of the greatest magnitude.
rated sinew Mainstay of great strength.
instant Immediate.
special head Finest troops.
mo corrivals More partners.
estimation Worth.
command Generalship.
to visit Euphemism: Henry would conduct mopping-up operations.
confederacy Conspiracy.

Revision questions on Act IV

1 Outline the bad news which the rebels receive during the Act.
2 Find quotations to illustrate the rising fortunes of the King.
3 What is Falstaff's attitude to recruiting?
4 Summarize the thoughts and feelings of the leading rebels on the night before the battle.
5 What would be lost if the scene with the Archbishop were omitted from a production of the play?

Act V Scene 1

Dawn on the day of the battle. Worcester and Vernon arrive in the King's camp for the parley, which had been arranged by Hotspur. Henry rebukes Worcester for provoking him to war and then proceeds to offer pardon and peace. Worcester pays lip-service to the offer, but in the next breath, and at length, denounces the King for his ingratitude and oppression. Henry replies that this is a feeble attempt to gloss over revolutionary zeal. The Prince of Wales intervenes to offer settlement of the matter by means of single combat with Hotspur, but the King refuses to give his permission for such an encounter. Worcester is sent back to Hotspur to put to him the King's proposals.

The Prince is sure that the terms will not be acceptable. Falstaff, viewing the battle with great trepidation, asks for the Prince's protection should he be downed in the fight. Hal tells him to say his prayers. Alone, Falstaff launches into a catechism about 'honour', of which he does not have a very high opinion.

Commentary

References to the 'sun's distemp'rature', the 'southern wind', 'tempest' and the 'blust'ring day' reflect the political disorder with which the play is imbued. Cosmic disturbance, consequent upon regicide, is an indication of Divine displeasure. Henry's wish that the rebels should cease behaving like 'exhaled' meteors and move in an 'obedient orb' is an expression of a need to see God's will re-established. This is a vain hope, of course, and Henry must live out the consequences of his action when he deposed Richard. The King wins the battle but his reign knows no peace and his personal life remains sorely troubled.

The 'punishment' of the rebels for their part in the usurpation is near at hand. In this sense, Henry may be seen as an instrument of Divine retribution – an ironic twist, but consistent with the workings of the Almighty. Worcester paints Henry as the cuckoo in the nest, without mentioning his own cuckoo-like propensities: Bolingbroke could not have deposed Richard without the help of the very people who now oppose him. Thus there was a whole nest-load of cuckoos seeking to oppress the 'nest' of kingship. The image cannot be stretched too far but a 'nest' may be associated with a healthy, 'natural' harmonious existence; not at all similar to the rebellious forces which overthrew Richard. Shakespeare's putting of this image into the mouth of Worcester has the effect of drawing attention to how far from the truth it is, despite its surface plausibility.

Worcester's suspicions about the King's offer of peace are understandable, but there is no overt reason in the text to doubt them. Indeed, from his position of strength there is little need for Henry to make these overtures. Hal's chivalrous challenge to Hostpur has the effect of concentrating our minds on their rivalry. It is noticeable, too, that the Prince pays Hotspur a generous tribute; thus we are invited to see Percy as a worthy competitor for greatness.

Falstaff's wry comment on Worcester and his cynical analysis of 'honour' give us interesting perspectives on the affairs of his betters. His soliloquy, which closes the scene, has become justly famous. It would be absurd to lift it out of context and make Shakespeare into an 'anti-war playwright'. Shakespeare never steps forward from his plays and presents us with his own view. What we have here is an opinion to set beside the heroics of the play: the weight we give it will depend on our personal feelings. Clearly it presents a truth, but not *the* truth.

distemp'rature Sickness. The sun has an unhealthy red colour.
southern wind Thought to be a bringer of disease.
play the trumpet Sound fanfares.
exhal'd Erratic.
prodigy Omen.
broached Proposed.
entertain Spend.
dislike Hostility.
chewet A pun: chattering jackdaw or meat-pie.
staff of office Worcester resigned the office of steward of the king's household.
posted Hastened.
place Position.
account Reckoning.
new-fall'n right Inheritance to the Dukedom of Lancaster, due to Bolingbroke because of the death of John of Gaunt.
injuries Abuses.
wanton Disordered.
sufferances Injuries.
To gripe . . . sway To grab the entire kingdom.
dangerous countenance Hostile looks.
younger Earlier.
articulate Enumerated, set forth.
face Put a good face on, to cover up.
fickle changelings Turncoats, who easily change their allegiances.
rub . . . elbow Hug themselves with glee.
hurlyburly innovation The commotion of revolution.
moody Desperate.
set off his head i.e. setting aside the guilt of this present enterprise.
Yet this This I must say.
dread . . . on us We have the power to exact fearful retribution.
office Duty.
Colossus Mighty statue. Like the one that stood astride the harbour at Rhodes.
pricks Urges.

pricks me on Ticks me off (on the list of the dead, after a battle).
set to a leg Attach a leg to the body again, after it has been cut off.
grief Pain.
A trim reckoning! A fine state of affairs!
insensible Not accessible to the senses.
Detraction Slander.
scutcheon A shield with the coat of arms of a dead nobleman, displayed at the funeral.
catechism A means of teaching, involving a question-and-answer technique.

Act V Scene 2

Treacherously, and with the reluctant support of Vernon, Worcester decides not to inform Hotspur of the King's 'liberal and kind offer'. But Hotspur is told that Prince Hal challenged him to single combat. In response to Hotspur's enquiry as to the manner of the challenging, Vernon gives a glowing description of the young Prince. Hotspur accepts the implied rivalry of the challenge and looks forward to battle. A messenger arrives to announce that the 'King comes on apace'.

Commentary

Hotspur is shown to be the victim of the machinations of Worcester, who has always had to bear the main guilt for the rebellion. This has the effect of relieving Hotspur of some of the blame: he might well be excused on the grounds which Worcester offers in this scene. Thus we concentrate on the forthcoming climax with the knowledge that Hal has a worthy opponent. Vernon's description of the manner of the challenge maintains the chivalric mood, which had been momentarily marred by the deceit of Worcester. Hotspur's response is appropriate. The stage is set for battle.

still Always.
Supposition He will always regard us with suspicion.
a wild trick Instinctive wildness.
sad Sadly, seriously.
like oxen . . . the nearer death i.e. we shall be like oxen being fattened for slaughter.
trespass Wrongdoings.
an adopted . . . privilege A nickname that gives him an advantage over other people.
spleen Rash temper.

live Are active.
spring Source.
mended Amended.
foreswearing Perjuring himself.
engag'd Held hostage.
draw short breath Either because of the physical effort of fighting, or short breaths, taken on the point of death.
tasking Presentation of the challenge.
proof of arms Test of skill at fighting; a duel.
Trimm'd up Decked out.
dispraising . . . with you Saying that he could not find words to praise you highly enough.
blushing cital Shamefacedly gave a recital of his own weaknesses.
envy Malice.
misconstru'd . . . wantonness His wildness so misunderstood.
wild a liberty Free and easy.
I will . . . my courtesy Spoken with menacing irony.
dial's Sundial's.
Still . . . an hour Still too long by an hour (Refers to a base life which only lasted an hour.)

Act V Scene 3

The Battle of Shrewsbury. There are a number of counterfeit 'kings' fighting; Douglas has come across one of them, who in reality is Sir Walter Blunt. Blunt is killed. Douglas resolves to go and find the real King.

Falstaff, so far, has managed to avoid injury, although most of his men have been killed. The Prince enters and urges Falstaff to lend him his sword. Falstaff offers the Prince his pistol, which is in its case. The pistol case is empty, its place taken by a bottle of sack. The Prince throws the bottle at Falstaff and then rejoins the fray. In the meantime, Falstaff claims to have killed Percy; Hal is not convinced.

Commentary

Shakespeare, to convey the impression of a battle, gives us two snippets of action: one serious, the other comic. The first sequence between Sir Walter and Douglas is fierce and heroic: in effect, a prelude to the saving of the king in the next scene. It also anticipates the meeting of Hal and Hotspur. Falstaff's comment on 'grinning honour' refers back to his 'catechism' and provides an anti-heroic slant on the action. The emphasis on this play is clearly in support of the heroic view, and before our thoughts can reflect for too long on the dead Sir Walter, we are plunged into the comic 'business' with the bottle of sack. Falstaff's callous remarks about his 'ragamuffins' further alienates him from our sympathies, although doubtless Elizabethans were less squeamish than our present age.

crossest me Cross my path.
Upon my head On my account.
Semblably furnish'd Equipped with similar arms to.
coats Tunics, often with embroidered arms.
scoring A pun. Either, 'wounding'; or, 'reckoning up a bill' at a tavern.
for the town's end Beggars took up position at the end of a town's main thoroughfare, by the gate.
Turk Gregory A composite 'character'. Turks were notorious for their ferocity and cruelty. Gregory is probably Pope Gregory XIII, who was believed to have been involved in the St Bartholomew's Day Massacre (1572) and to have plotted the assassination of Elizabeth I.
carbonado Portion of sliced pork.

Act V Scene 4

This is the climax of the battle. The Prince is wounded but refuses to retire, despite the King's entreaties. Hal praises the endeavours of his younger brother, John of Lancaster. Douglas enters and immediately attacks the King, whose life is threatened. Hal defends his father and drives off Douglas.

Now Hotspur and Hal confront each other: they fight and eventually Hotspur is slain. Hal speaks an epitaph over the body of Hotspur and then notices Falstaff, who is also apparently dead. After saying farewell to his erstwhile companion, Hal leaves Falstaff lying beside Hotspur. But things are not as they seem: feeling that it is now safe to do so, Falstaff 'rises up' – he has been feigning death. He catches sight of Hotspur, stabs him in the thigh, puts him on his back and claims him as his victim. Prince John and Hal re-enter to be faced with Falstaff, who demands reward for his supposed feat of arms. John, not surprisingly, regards this as 'the strangest tale' he has ever heard. Hal is not disposed to deny Falstaff the credit for killing Hotspur. The rebels sound the retreat and Falstaff, yet again, vows reform.

Commentary

The scene begins by establishing that the Prince has been wounded in the battle; thus we admire his courage in refusing to withdraw and see him at a disadvantage when the time comes to fight with Hotspur. The keynote of this scene is to be undivided admiration for Prince Hal. In paying a compliment to his brother, Prince John, Hal is seen now as one who can recognize honour in others. Previously in council, John had taken the place of the Prince of Wales: now Hal has accepted the position of superiority.

The King's rescue by Hal demonstrates dramatically the loyalty which previously the King had questioned. During the 'interview-scene' Henry had envisaged the possibility that Hal would have fought against him. This proposition is here answered.

Although the fight between Hal and Hotspur takes place in battle, it has all the hall-marks of a chivalric encounter. It begins formally with both combatants identifying themselves – not using their titles – as men: Harry Monmouth, Harry Percy. Hal then calls himself by his title 'Prince of Wales', this indicating full acceptance of his role, with all it entails. Finally, before the fighting begins, the Prince reminds us of the intention which was expressed at the end of Act I Scene 2. The vow he made then, and later to his father, is about to be fulfilled.

During the contest, there is a mock-fight between Douglas and Falstaff which forms an ironic commentary on the battle between Hal and Hotspur. Again, Shakespeare, even at this moment, wishes to keep in our minds that momentous events have a comic parallel. This is a daring stroke and one may justly wonder what Shakespeare intends. It would seem to go against the grain of the play to see this episode as indicating that Shakespeare is belittling the truly heroic encounter. Clearly the episode does diminish Douglas, whose fiery temperament has its ludicrous side. In passing, we may notice that although everybody pays lip-service to the valour of Douglas, it is mildly amusing that we first hear of him defeated by Hotspur, and later he is seen lashing out at counterfeit kings. Also, Hal sends him running. The only success of Douglas would seem to be 'killing' Falstaff – and he can't even do that job properly. Douglas seems to represent a sort of mindless violence which is not really worthy of much respect.

Hotspur's death is moving not only because he acknowledges gracefully that the Prince has deprived him of all his 'proud titles', but also because Shakespeare makes us feel a sense of loss for a young man in his prime ('O Harry, thou hast robbed me of my youth!'). This represents a culmination of something that we have always felt about Hotspur: he had his public and sometimes exasperating aspect, always talking about his 'honour' etc., but Shakespeare kept before us the human side of the young man – particularly in those moments which he enjoyed with Kate.

The Prince's epitaph over Hotspur is magnanimous. It begins by finishing the sentence which Hotspur had begun: a touching moment. The stress of the Prince's tribute to his rival is not upon the act of rebellion, which is allowed to sleep with Hotspur in the grave; instead, Hal concentrates on the passing of an essentially noble spirit. There is no crowing over the defeat of an enemy, no self-congratulation.

In its way, the Prince's epitaph over the shamming Falstaff is almost as generous. The puns need cause us no disquiet: they are in harmony with the relationship which we have witnessed between them – the language of chivalry for Hotspur, the repartee of the tavern softened for Falstaff. In both tributes Shakespeare lets us feel that the Prince is personally involved – neither is perfunctory.

The rising of Falstaff from the dead is, of course, one of the great comic moments in Shakespeare. It is worth remembering that an audience, suspending disbelief at this juncture, actually supposes Falstaff to be dead. Thus we may be entitled to claim an element of surprise for the moment. This might be stressed by the actor delaying the resurrection for a few seconds, and making the revival gradual rather than sudden. Falstaff's words on recovery are predictable: he values life at any price. His stabbing of Hotspur's dead body cannot be other than reprehensible, and the claim that he has killed him is so outrageous that the Prince, safe in the knowledge that no one will believe it, is content to 'gild' the deception. It is perhaps noteworthy that Hal is not concerned with personal glorification – a lesser man might well have felt affronted by Falstaff's audacity and consequently been unable to restrain giving vent to outrage.

make up Go forward.
amaze Alarm.
stain'd Blood-stained.
breathe Pause for breath.
at the point At the point of his sword.
ungrown Inexperienced.
Hydra A many-headed snake-like monster, slain by Hercules. It grew two heads for each one cut off.
assay Test in battle.
injury Slander.

Two . . . sphere Each star was supposed to move in its own orbit, according to the Ptolemaic view of the universe.
name Reputation.
vanities Empty boats.
the slave . . . fool Thoughts are dependent on life, and life itself is the plaything of time.
stout Brave.
sensible Able to be aware of.
favours This refers to Prince Hal's heraldic device, ostrich plumes.
ignominy Shame.
deer Another pun, this time on 'deer'/'dear'.
Embowell'd Disembowelled, prior to being embalmed; or, in the case of a deer, prior to being salted and spiced for venison.
powder Salt.
termagant Name of a bloodthirsty Mohammedan deity, familiar to Shakespeare's audience as a character in Morality Plays.
paid Killed.
scot and lot With a clean sweep.
Nothing . . . eyes Only an eye-witness could prove me a liar.
flesh'd Blooded for the first time.
Jack Rogue.
gild it Make it appear genuine, vouch for it.

Act V Scene 5

Having won the battle, the King proceeds to judge the rebels. He condemns immediately Worcester and Vernon but defers sentence on the remainder. The Prince asks to be responsible for Douglas. The King grants his request, at which Prince Hal graciously gives his brother John the responsibility of setting the Scotsman free. The King then resolves to divide his army so that they may march upon those rebels who remain. John and Westmoreland are ordered to meet Northumberland and Scroop. Henry himself, together with the Prince, will advance towards Wales to confront Glendower and Mortimer. The King looks forward to a time when England will be purged of rebellion.

Commentary

Henry is rigorous in his judgement of Worcester and Vernon, but his leniency in refusing to sentence the remainder before consideration reveals a merciful streak. The feeling at the end of the play is that the King's family has achieved harmony: Henry is obviously in charge, the Prince is at one with the father, and

John is deferring to his elder brother. The fact is, of course, that rebellion has not been obliterated and the final lines look forward to a renewal of armed struggle. The defeat of rebellion must await *Henry IV Part 2*.

rebuke Check. The King apparently does not have in mind his own rebellion against Richard II.
ill-spirited Malicious.
turn . . . contrary Say our offers were the opposite of what they really were.
tenor Nature, conditions.
intelligence Information.
pause Defer sentence.
Upon the foot of fear Fleeing in fear.
bounty Act of generosity.
give way Act upon.
leave Hesitate.

Revision questions on Act V

1 Why does Worcester decide to deceive Hotspur over the King's peace overtures?
2 Outline the main events of the Battle of Shrewsbury.
3 Why do you think that the King refused to allow the Prince to fight Hotspur in single combat?
4 Can you account for Hal's apparent unwillingness to take the credit for killing Hotspur?
5 Comment on the King's handling of the situation after his victory.
6 Discuss Shakespeare's portrayal of the Prince in this Act. What effect do you think he is trying to achieve and do you find it successful?
7 What influence does Falstaff's catechism on honour have on your understanding of the events in this Act?
8 Show the dramatic importance of Falstaff's conduct during the battle.
9 Discuss the importance of (a) Douglas, (b) Vernon, (c) Sir Walter Blunt in Act V.
10 How far do you find that Hotspur engages your sympathies in Act V? Give reasons for your answer.

Shakespeare's art in *Henry IV Part 1*

Setting and date

The play deals with events of the early fifteenth century, but the immediate setting of the play is Elizabethan England. The tavern is clearly an Elizabethan hostelry. The play *King Cambyses* to which Falstaff refers was first performed in about 1569. There are other such anachronisms as references to the high cost of oats, the 'watch' and psalm-singing weavers. Fifteenth century history is given a distinctly Elizabethan flavour!

Henry IV Part 1 is one of eight plays of Shakespeare which concern the period of English history between the reign of Richard II and the accession of Henry VII. It was first performed in the mid-1590s and a printed edition appeared in 1598. It is tempting to think that Shakespeare chose this period of history as a subject for drama because of its topicality for his audience. Elizabeth was in her sixties and there was much anxiety about who was to succeed her. With no clear-cut heir available there was the worry that on her death the country might be plunged into factionalism and civil war, as rival claimants struggled for power. Past experience had taught that chaos was the result when the monarchy was weak or did not enjoy universally-acknowledged legitimacy. *Henry IV Part 1* (and the other History Plays) demonstrate the disorder which is consequent upon a weak monarch, or one whose title is open to question.

Themes

Order and disorder, the historical theme

To orthodox medieval philosophers, the universe and everything in it was an ordered structure, created and presided over by God. Each constituent of this cosmos had a fixed rank, or value, and fulfilled a function according to the dictates of Divine Providence. The structure was thus hierarchial: at the top of the pyramid was the Creator, beneath came the Angels, next Man, and so on down the scale until one reached the humblest forms of inanimate matter. Each broad hierarchy was thought to be sub-divided into other hierarchies and the whole was dependent upon its parts.

In the beginning all Creation was harmonious: God reigned in Heaven. Man, in his rank below the Angels, was Lord of the Earth. The whole proclaimed the glory of the Creator. Unfortunately, by misuse of the gift of free-will the harmony between Man and God was broken – discord entered the world, as the result of sin. Man, or a man, might regain his favoured position in the Divine Scheme by virtue of God's grace, but he had to be continually on his guard lest he once again fall into sin, by giving way to his 'lower', or bestial self. The consequences of such a falling-off were manifestly horrendous, and affected not only the individual sinner but also had ramifications in the world around him. The more eminent the sinner, the more profound the sin, so the consequences were the more dire.

The king occupied the chief position in the hierarchy of the nation. He rules the state by Divine Right – he was God's bailiff on earth. To overthrow and kill the rightful king was thus conceived as an act of sacrilege and invited the direst punishment from the Almighty. The usurper, inevitably, would come to experience Divine justice and the nation could expect no peace until the will of God was re-established. In extreme circumstances, the very fabric of the heavens might become disordered: strange eclipses, comets, tempests were often supposed to be manifestations of Divine displeasure.

Tudor historians, adopting the orthodox standpoint, believed that history demonstrated the working of God's justice and His vengeance. The period from the reign of Richard II to the death of Richard III was thought to reveal the working of Divine

Providence. Richard II, a 'bad' king, nevertheless was God's anointed ruler. Henry Bolingbroke, in deposing him committed sacrilege, and, as a consequence was punished by civil unrest. There was a brief moment of respite under the rule of Henry V, but the whole country was plunged into the Wars of the Roses during the reign of Henry VI. Richard III, himself a regicide, purged the nation of the guilt of Bolingbroke's original crime, before perishing himself at Bosworth. Finally, God's Providence was reasserted by the accession of Henry Tudor, a 'rightful' successor – and greatness was restored to the kingdom. By this means, a neat, schematic and propagandist interpretation is given to the chaos and bloodletting subsequent upon the usurpation of Richard II.

If we come now to *Henry IV Part 1*, it will be evident that it is possible to see the play as an exemplification of the Tudor view of events. Bolingbroke appears as a man weighed down by the guilt of his crime. Now Henry IV, he reigns over a threatening realm, which is shortly to erupt into civil war. The allies, who aided his usurpation, no longer are to be trusted and the bonds of allegiance have been weakened to breaking-point. Just as the 'family of the nation' is insecure, so also the King's own family is subject to mistrust – the father doubts the loyalty of the son. Also, the lower orders of society itself do not appear to 'know their place': Falstaff sees himself as possibly enjoying a position of eminence in the state. The Prince of Wales consorts with the common people. Crime flourishes both on a grand scale and in the petty reaches of society. The King's highway is unsafe and subject to the depradations of the heir to the throne himself, With the help of his son, Henry is able to achieve a degree of stability within the country, but he appears again in *Henry IV Part 2* as a sickly and troubled king ruling a sickly and troubled nation. As we have said there is a brief moment of glory under Henry V, not a usurper, before the onset of the Wars of the Roses.

Thus it is possible to see the play as a working-out of the Tudor view of history, but it needs to be stressed that Shakespeare is writing drama, not history. The characters and themes which he explores have a life of their own, and refuse to be neatly schematized. Obviously, for example, it would be ludicrous to pretend that Henry is an incapable king. Our analysis of his character and deeds show that in many ways he is well-suited to the role. Certainly, he has more secular 'qualifications' than the appallingly weak Richard II. True, he lacks the Divine sanction for rule and there are many suggestion that this is his fatal flaw. Rather than force our interest to focus on the conventional view of Henry as the usurper, who lives out the consequences of his sin, Shakespeare directs our attention on the man himself – this is, of course, the manner of the true dramatist. Thus Henry is not so much an exemplification of doctrine, but more a man who faces a dilemma: he seeks to be a good king, but is forced to use nefarious means to achieve his goal. Once he is crowned, he would like to rule efficiently and beneficently, but he is dogged by his past. He cannot escape the fact that he is a 'counterfeit king'.

There are few, if any, direct references to Providence in the play: Glendower mentions the prodigies which greeted his birth – but these are scorned by Hotspur, with whom one feels we are invited to agree. Falstaff, in giving expression constantly to a cynical, worldly view of events (great and small) seems in his massive person to stand opposed to any grand view of the world.

On the evidence of this play, therefore, it would appear that Shakespeare is more interested in giving expression to the variety and contradictions of the human predicament, rather than presenting a narrowly doctrinaire interpretation of events.

The honour theme

Hotspur sees honour in terms of military prowess: it is the respect which comes from the performance of heroic deeds on the field of battle. Honour is the reputation for chivalry which may be achieved by setting free the captured Douglas. Hotspur, according to the King, is 'the very theme of honour's tongue' and all that we see of him seems to conform this opinion. This 'swaddling Mars' cannot resist a challenge – the more dangerous the better. Hotspur is not content with some of the glory that may be on offer, he wants all of it: he brooks no rival. When he clashes with Glendower over the question of the division of the spoils of war, he will not compromise and 'cavils' until he gets his way. Once his reputation for driving a hard bargain is established, then he is prepared to give way and thus accentuate his reputation for magnanimity.

In contrast to Hotspur, Falstaff scorns the very notion of honour as a motive for human action. To him it is a mere word that has no practical use and is soon diminished once its possessor is dead. Essentially the pursuit of honour is destructive:

Who hath it? He that died a Wednesday. Doth he feel it? No. Doth he hear it? No. 'Tis insensible then? Yea, to the dead. But will it not live with the living? No. Why? Detraction will not suffer it. Therefore I'll none of it.

Falstaff values survival above intangible honour. He would rather live a coward than die a hero. The 'grinning honour' of the dead Sir Walter provokes the comment, 'Give me life; which if I can save, so; if not, honour comes unlooked for, and there's an end.'

As we might expect, Hal's concept of honour is more subtle than that of either Falstaff or Hotspur. For a time he is prepared to forgo the Hotspur version altogether and he mixes with those who can only stain his reputation as the heir apparent. But he is also prepared to see Hotspur's honour as a prize which he intends to wrest from him. Thus, to Hal, honour is a means to an end; not, as for Hotspur, and end in itself. It will obviously be useful for Hal to possess it once he needs it, but until such time he can afford to pursue his education in the tavern – secure in the knowledge that the unwitting Hotspur is garnering up honour on his behalf.

To some extent, Hal may be seen as occupying the middle ground. He does not share Falstaff's cynical view that honour is worthless, but he is realistic enough to see it for what it is worth.

The characters

Prince Hal

We first hear of Prince Hal from his father, who in the mould of many fathers before and since, is bemoaning the waywardness of his son. At a time when civil war threatens the state, the heir to the throne is apparently wasting his time in Eastcheap – in the company of a fat, ageing knight called Falstaff. To make matters even more hurtful for the King, the rebellious faction has as one of its leaders a most valiant young man, Harry Percy, who is the very 'theme of honour's tongue'. How unlike Harry, Prince of Wales, whose brow is stained with 'riot and dishonour'.

At first sight, the behaviour of the Prince would seem to confirm the unfavourable opinion of his father: he is in the tavern with Falstaff; the subject of their conversation is highway robbery; indeed, before the scene has ended, Hal has agreed to partake in an escapade which involves theft from innocent travellers at Gad's Hill. Overall, emanating principally from Falstaff, the scene is permeated by an atmosphere of time-wasting, lawlessness and self-indulgence. It is not surprising that Hotspur feels contemptuous of Hal, dismissing him as 'that same sword-and-buckler Prince of Wales'.

However, the King, Hotspur and Falstaff are wrong about the Prince. By the end of the play, Hal will be united with his father; Hotspur will be killed in battle by the sword of the Prince of Wales; Falstaff will have been relegated to the sidelines of the Prince's life. And the audience knows from virtually the beginning of the play that Hal's reputation does not reflect the real young man.

Of course, Shakespeare's audience would have been conversant with the legendary wildness of the young Prince, who was to reform and become the heroic, warrior-king personified: Henry V. The central interest of the play is Shakespeare's portrayal of the transformation of the 'madcap' into true princeliness. Hal's soliloquy at the end of Act I, Scene 2 is of key importance: it clearly demonstrates that all we have witnessed hitherto, and much that we shall see hereafter, is a performance. Whatever the King, Falstaff, Hotspur and others may think of Hal's behaviour, the truth is that he understands himself and the nature of his destiny:

I know you all, and will awhile uphold
The unyoked humour of your idleness.

Thus the Prince establishes the transience of his wildness. Falstaff and his other cronies may think that they enjoy the fellowship of the heir to the throne, but their intimacy is to be short-lived – and on the Prince's terms. The 'loose behaviour' is to be cast off like an old garment, to reveal the true man beneath it, and the intention is that the reformation will be the more marvelled at because of its unexpectedness. Some callousness is evident here. Hal is obviously prepared, for the sake of his greater glory, to mislead Falstaff and his father. We need not lose too much sleep over the deception of Falstaff, but his father's unhappiness, together with the disunity which is bred at court, needs greater justification. Shakespeare's answer is to present Hal as a young man who is self-consciously aware that the demands of kingship entail more than moving solely in the predictable court circles. At the beginning of Act II, Scene 4 he tells Poins that he has 'sounded the very base-string of humility . . . I am sworn brother to a leash of drawers, and can call them all by their christen names, as Tom, Dick and Francis.' Here Hal is declaring the successful outcome of an experiment: he has managed to humble himself sufficiently for the basest in the kingdom to regard him as one of themselves. Such behaviour is clearly calculated, but not merely to give him the cheap satisfaction of hoodwinking unintelligent drawers. Its intention, as Hal implies later in the speech, is that he may get to know the world of the lower orders, for one day 'when I am king of England I shall command all the good lads in Eastcheap.'

So far as Hotspur is concerned, the Prince is equally calculating: no attempt is made to outdo his rival, until they face each other at Shrewsbury. Again Hal's intentions are plainly stated, this time to his father:

the time will come,
That I shall make this northern youth exchange
His glorious deeds for my indignities.

In this sense, Hal sees Hotspur as his 'factor', employed to gather up honour on behalf of his master, only to hand it over 'in the closing of some glorious day'. In the meantime, Hal is free to pursue his studies amidst low company.

One can only marvel at the Prince's efficiency. Events turn out exactly as he has planned. Before we discuss the apotheosis of Hal, let us examine Shakespeare's presentation of his low-life behaviour in a little more detail. Hal's actions are in line with his stated policy. For example, the Gad's Hill robbery is indulged in for enjoyment, not profit, and Shakespeare carefully distances the Prince from the innocent victims of the crime. Hal robs Falstaff, not the travellers, and he takes care to see that the money is paid back with interest. The booty is the discomfiture of Falstaff and the Prince is even prepared to protect him from the law – for the time being at least. Much of the 'loose talk' which transpires between Falstaff and Hal shows the fat knight to be the initiator, whilst the Prince keeps himself in reserve. This is particularly noticeable during their opening exchange in Act I, and in the famous scene when the mock-interview between the King and his son is 'staged' in the tavern. Typically, the idea of having a 'play extempore' on the subject of 'when thou comest to thy father' is Falstaff's. Whilst Falstaff plays the King, the jest can be maintained, but it is not long before the Prince suggests that the roles be reversed. Now that Hal is 'king' the atmosphere changes and Falstaff finds himself trapped and having to listen to a scathing denunciation of his failings. His defence is good, but culminates in an appeal about which there is a note of poignancy beneath the bluster: 'Banish plump Jack, and banish all the world.' Hal's reply, after what we may imagine a moment of dramatic pause, is unequivocal: 'I do, I will.' What are we to make of this episode which looks forward to the real interview with the King? It seems to exemplify much of the nature of the relationship between Hal and Falstaff: at times when the jest seems to be going too far, then the Prince frequently, though not always so explicitly, drags Falstaff and himself back to the realities which he has already shown himself to recognize. This accounts for the slightly uneasy mirth which is apparent in Act I, Scene 2 (*Falstaff*: 'Do not when thou art king hang a thief.' *Prince*: 'No, thou shalt.'). It is always apparent that the Prince never gives himself over entirely to the ways of Falstaff: he maintains the upper hand in whatever situation he finds himself. The actor and the role do not become one. In the telling moment, during the 'play extempore', Hal does identify absolutely with the part he is playing: he becomes 'King' and Falstaff is denounced and renounced, which will be his ultimate fate at the end of *Henry IV Part 2*.

The awareness that Hal's frivolity is to some extent contrived undeniably detracts from his attractiveness as a character: we like people to be what they seem. But in Hal's defence it may be suggested that kings can never be what they seem. It is part of the nature of kingship which Shakespeare explores explicitly in *Henry V* that a king 'is but a man', but yet cannot be as other men: such is the penalty of kingship. Far from antagonizing us towards Hal, it is conceivable that we should see a certain pathos in Hal's situation. Here, Shakespeare presents us with a naturally high-spirited young man who is undeniably attracted to a life which he must exchange one day for the frigidities of the court. For a fleeting moment he is able to enjoy the freedoms of Eastcheap, but always at the back of his mind is the knowledge that such liberty cannot ultimately be his.

Hal had cultivated an air of amused detachment whenever Hotspur's name had been mentioned:

he that kills me some six or seven dozen of Scots
at a breakfast, washes his hands, and says to his
wife, 'Fie upon this quiet life! I want work . . .'

Hal's portrayal is satirical and exact; until he 'is of Percy's mind' he affects to be unconcerned about the fearsomeness of his rival's reputation. As the moment of actual confrontation draws near, so Hal shows Hotspur the more respect, which reaches its climax as they prepare to do battle:

Two stars keep not their motion in one sphere,
Nor can one England brook a double reign
Of Harry Percy and the Prince of Wales.

By this time the Prince has attained undoubted chivalric dignity and is fulfilling the role which fate has determined for him. This aspect of the Prince had already made itself apparent to Vernon, who described him thus:

I saw young Harry with his beaver on,
. . .
Rise from the ground like feathered Mercury . . .

That Hal may be described in these terms, after his dealings in Eastcheap, should not surprise us: it has been part of Shakespeare's understanding of the man that this was the 'real' Prince all along. We admire the courage with which Hal faces up to his valiant competitor and we are moved by the magnanimity of the words which he speaks over Hotspur's dead body. The tribute is free from all self-congratulation, modest and sincere:

Adieu, and take thy praise to Heaven.
Thy ignominy sleep with thee in the grave,
Be not remembered in thy epitaph.

It will be apparent that Shakespeare has taken the myth which surrounded the early days of Prince Hal, and shaped it to give a picture of a young man coming to terms with his destiny. On the surface, we see the progress from irresponsibility to the moment of reformation. Shakespeare's reworking of the familiar story starts from the premise that Hal was never really irresponsible: his wildness was a pretence, a consciously adopted role which he played in order that he might become the more effective king. At the end of the play, as he predicted, we see that he has taken possession of the high renown which formerly belonged to Hotspur. Every glory has been rendered up. We have also seen how his foray into the lower reaches of society has enabled him to familiarize himself with the ways and thoughts of those over whom one day he will have 'command'. This will be no 'ivory tower' king. Finally, he has achieved mastery over himself: the 'old Adam' which lurks within all humanity has been faced, in the shape of Falstaff – but there has been no compromise, no surrender.

Falstaff

Falstaff is one of the best-loved of all Shakespeare's characters, and yet we ought to revile him. In many ways his actions and attitudes are deplorable: he is given to sensual indulgence, he lies, he steals, he refuses to pay his bills, he is a bully, he has no sense of honour, he exploits the weak, he values his own skin at any price – and yet we are bewitched by him. He is also a coward.

Falstaff represents all that is antithetical to good order. In the course of his opening dialogue with Hal (much of which is concerned with the joys of highway robbery), Falstaff eagerly looks forward to the time when Hal is king. He anticipates, as a reward for the friendship he has shown the Prince, becoming 'a brave judge'. One can only speculate that the kingdom in which Falstaff held judicial powers would, in reality, be devoid of all justice: a state which enshrined topsy-turvy moral values. It is comforting indeed that Hal brushes aside such a grim fantasy. But Falstaff defies conventions: he has no truck with the received opinions about 'honour', remarking with a candour with which we can have some sympathy, that 'honour' is a mere word – as insubstantial as the breath which utters it. It is also a convention that old men should display 'gravity', or, at at the very least, act as if they were old and not pretend to be young.

But if Falstaff's order is in fact disorder, it need not surprise us that he defies this convention, too.

Falstaff's cowardice is blatant at the Battle of Shrewsbury, and in his running away as soon as real opposition presents itself at Gad's Hill. In the catastrophe of this latter episode, perhaps we can admire the audacious fibs which he tells in order to escape from the trap which Hal and Poins have laid for him. It is more difficult to find attractive his attempt to deprive the good-hearted hostess of the money which he owes her. We cannot but find his treatment of the 'scarecrows' who must fight for him callous and distasteful. Along with his enormities, Falstaff adopts an attitude of mock-piety. He is adept at quoting Scripture for his own purposes; he constantly vows that he will reform and mend his ways. So deeply disordered is his whole way of life that we know such gestures carry no conviction. His vast bulk seems to personify ungoverned appetite.

From a functional point of view Falstaff represents the 'riot and dishonour' with which the Prince is supposedly stained. In microscosm he shows us what the kingdom might become under an unregenerate Hal. Inevitably, he must be rejected, for he has no place in the well-governed realm of Henry V. Final rejection does come at the end of *Henry IV Part 2* and this is prefigured in this play in Act II, Scene 4. Acting the part of the King, Falstaff offers us his version of reality: naturally and characteristically, he claims virtue for himself (thus reversing the moral reality) and implies that, although Hal may justly banish all other acquaintances, he must cleave to 'sweet Jack Falstaff, kind Jack Falstaff, true Jack Falstaff, valiant Jack Falstaff, and therefore the more valiant being as he is, old Jack Falstaff'. To banish him the Prince must banish all the world. The Prince's emphatic rejection of Falstaff's world establishes the proper moral perspective, and from this moment his influence, such as it was, over Hal declines: he is no longer the centre of Hal's life and he is shortly to utter a mock-lament for his dwindling girth, which may well match his dwindling fortunes. Critics have remarked on the affinity between Shakespeare's Falstaff and the character Vice in the medieval Morality Plays. In these plays, Virtue was tempted by the blandishments of Vice, only to return to the true path in the end. It is possible to see this pattern mirrored in the relationship between Hal and Falstaff. In rejecting Falstaff, therefore, Hal may be seen to reject that part of his own personality which threatens his own moral integrity.

As we have seen, the case against Falstaff is strong but it would be absurd to ignore his power to captivate us. Part of his attraction lies in the fact that we find him so much fun. Quite simply, he invigorates us by his very presence – he is Shakespeare's supreme comic creation and we are prepared to love anybody who makes us laugh. There is comedy to be found in his physical aspect and many jokes arise from this source: if he is 'down' then he will require 'levers' to raise him up again. Then there is his outrageous wit: he is never at a loss for an answer. The Prince has him trapped in his own web of exaggeration when he claims to have been hopelessly outnumbered on Gad's Hill, but Falstaff can find a 'starting-hole' into which he can escape: 'By the Lord, I knew ye as well as he that made ye.'

For sheer verbal dexterity Falstaff has no equal: he is a mine of puns, he can give vent to a vivid stream of abuse, he twists Scripture to suit his own devices. He is immensely resourceful. His playing of the role of Henry IV is beautifully judged – to suit himself, whilst damning all others. The speech on 'honour', rightly famed, counterbalances the inflated views of Hotspur, and not least, has the virtue of making us think. Somehow we feel he can't be right, but what is the flaw in his argument? Falstaff carries about with him a sense of the unexpected, we never quite know what he is going to say or do. Having been forced to fight on the King's side, and gathered about him his band of scarecrows, who could have predicted that he would crown his military career with the glory of killing the redoubtable Hostpur?

Falstaff's lack of principles enables him to debunk the principles of others, and the wholehearted way in which he does so enables him to get away with it. That he can be so outrageously good-humoured, whilst saying and doing outrageous things, and still command our love, is perhaps his greatest escape of all.

King Henry IV

At the outset we see a king who is beset by troubles. He is sick of soul because of the guilt he bears for the usurpation and death of Richard II, the rightful king. Former friends, who had helped him to his present eminence, are now disaffected and threatening open revolt. To make matters worse his eldest son seems careless of his responsibilities – hardly a fitting heir to the dearly-won throne. Yet, despite the difficulties, he is determined to rule.

When he meets the rebellious faction at Windsor, Henry puts

forth a regal manner and peremptorily dismisses Worcester from the council chamber. This is impressive: Henry may have inner uncertainties, but he is not going to be intimidated. To Hotspur, the King is 'a fawning greyhound' and a practitioner of 'vile policy', and from what we see of Henry, there may well be some appropriateness about this opinion. Certainly, it is evident that he possesses what may be termed 'a calculating habit of mind'. A high degree of political awareness, by the King's own admission, was revealed by the manner in which he wooed the populace to his side, and away from Richard. Even his projected crusade has a political dimension in helping to distract from dissension at home.

When the time comes Henry can act decisively: once he has been convinced of Hal's loyalty, then immediately he is put in a post of responsibility and preparations for war are launched:

Our hands are full of business. Let's away:
Advantage feeds him fat while men delay.

There is no evidence of weakness here: opposition puts him on his mettle and brings out the best in him.

Before the battle the King shrewdly refuses to allow the Prince to engage in single combat with Hostpur: he is too canny to risk everything on one throw of the dice. His offer to come to terms with his opponents is also politically sound: if it is accepted then he negotiates from a position of strength, if it is refused then he will have gained moral stature by his apparent willingness to be reasonable. He must know that it is more than likely he is going to win. Likewise, after dealing summarily with Worcester and Vernon, he gains by his intention to 'pause' before settling with the remainder of his defeated enemies. Mindful of his public image, he obviously intends to win the peace.

The King's private life is integrated with his public self. It would not be true to say that he is ineffectual before his relationship with Hal is established, but it is evident that he is given new heart by the understanding which arises during the 'interview scene'. If we compare the nagging fretfulness of his opening speeches with what he says after Hal has made his loyalty clear, it would appear that 'conversion' would not be too strong a word:

A hundred thousand rebels die in this!
Thou shalt have charge and sovereign trust herein.

Only moments before he had been suggesting the possibility that Hal would be fighting for the rebel cause.

Loyalty has been the King's primary concern. The usurper is

not in a position to lay claim to the loyalty of those who helped him to the throne, but as a father he may expect the loyalty of his son. Once this family bond is asserted by Hal, then Henry can naturally draw strength from it: at least his son's supposed disloyalty is not to be reckoned as one of God's punishments for his 'mistreadings'. The royal family is secure but the problem still remains of the allegiance of the larger 'family' of the nation. To achieve stability the King must inevitably rely upon force.

Hotspur

As the fortunes of Harry Plantagenet rise in the play, so those of Harry Percy diminish. The King juxtaposes the two young men very early in the play: we see them as competitors: comparisons are invited.

Hotspur immediately strikes us as an heroic young man. Whilst Hal has been in Eastcheap, Hotspur has been fighting against the Scots and has emerged triumphant. The King's opinion of his merit ('the theme of honour's tongue') is thus confirmed. Stress is laid (mainly by himself) on Hotspur's physical prowess in battle and his blunt, soldierly nature is exemplified by his contemptuous description of the King's 'popinjay', who demanded prisoners. Hand them over he would not. Ironically, he is forced to hand over more than a few Scots to Prince Hal on a later occasion. Hotspur is affronted by the niceties of court behaviour and impetuously, and somewhat understandably, defies the King.

Hotspur's tendency to act first and think afterwards makes him ideal material for the scheming Worcester to act upon, and even at the outset of the play we see him using Hotspur's sense of outrage for devious purposes. Frequently Hotspur simply erupts. Fortunately, from our point of view, although he professes to abominate 'mincing poetry', Hotspur gives vent to many displays of verbal pyrotechnics. It seems that his spirit simply cannot be contained – his striking metaphors, whilst they may lack discipline, lend great vividness to his portrayal:

By heaven methinks it were an easy leap,
To pluck bright honour from the pale-faced moon . . .

Face to face with the also poetical, but more mystical Glendower, the two personalities clash; Hotspur's poeticism is of a fairly narrow range, and focuses mainly upon battles, fighting in general and especially upon his honour. Also it is a poetry of extremes: anger, contempt, courage – all expressed with the utmost vigour.

Hotspur's sense of honour is tied in with his self-esteem, but it is most important to him that others should recognize it and show due deference whenever it is in question. His vanity will not allow him even to appear to be getting the worst of a deal, so much so that he will pretend to be a victim of injustice, even when he is not. Hence he pushes Glendower, whom he sees as a rival, almost to breaking-point over the relatively trivial matter of a small tract of land. But once he has won his point he gives the land back to his rival. Caution might have dictated a less risky course: conciliation in the larger interests of factional unity. But Hotspur is a creature of impulse: he divulges the plot to a friend, only to realize later that he has probably divulged the rebel plans to a person who will betray them to the King.

As the play unfolds it becomes clear that Hotspur would make a disastrous ruler of a kingdom. We have seen how Hal rarely puts a foot wrong (despite appearances); in contrast Hotspur is very error-prone. He jeopardizes the harmony of the conspirators by his lack of political judgement, he is inefficient and forgets a vital map, he underestimates his adversaries, he cannot see through Worcester's machinations and he is vain. But he is not a villain. For all his faults, we see him as a likeable person. In his relationship with his wife, we see his humorous, 'softer' side: he chides her for her ineffectual oaths, and there is a pathos as we see their love subjected to the tensions of war. He is generous and fiercely loyal to Douglas, a former enemy. We cannot blame him for being wrong about Hal, but one wonders, had he killed Hal, if his tribute would have been quite so generous. But it would be wrong to see Hotspur as a mere injudicious ranter. For all his flights of fancy there is sometimes evident a down-to-earth, commonsensical realism in his nature: he earns our applause in his putting-down of Glendower, and his anti-romanticism is refreshing when he talks with Kate or good-naturedly exposes the sugariness of Mortimer and his incomprehensible Welsh wife.

Because of his flamboyant public persona, other people tend to be deceived by Hotspur. He is judged, like Hal, by appearances. He appears to be the very soul of honour and military prowess, but from what we learn from Kate this may not be the whole truth. She speaks of a Hotspur who is not sleeping, who is subject to nightmares and moments of abstraction – all symptoms of inner unease and, perhaps, guilt. Hotspur is not given to overt self-doubt, but it does not require much psychological insight to suspect that Shakespeare is portraying a young man, whose very certainties and refusal to put his honour to any scrutiny, is in reality covering up a troubled mind.

The truly wayward spirit in the play is Hotspur, not Hal. The Prince is consistent, whereas Hotspur is anarchic. For all his great gifts Hotspur is flawed: he has a speech impediment, he has a divided self, he is disruptive within his own circle, and he is in the final analysis a rebel who threatens to disrupt all England.

In fairness to Hotspur, it may be noted that as the play develops so he becomes more considered in his judgements. Realizing that the odds are against him before the battle, he shows a brave determination to face them, whatever the outcome may be – he does not take refuge in fantasy, pretending that things are other than they are:

Let each man do his best; and here draw I
A sword whose temper I intend to stain
With the best blood that I can meet withal
In the adventure of this perilous day . . .

Also, he is prepared to give some consideration to the King's offer of peace.

Worcester

Worcester is the arch-villian of the rebel cause. Insolently, he provokes the King to dismiss him from the council chamber at Windsor Castle and then loses no time in persuading Northumberland and Hotspur to lend themselves to this scheme. His deviousness is self-proclaimed by the terminology he uses: Northumberland shall 'secretly into the bosom creep/ Of that same noble prelate well-beloved,/ The Archbishop'. Worcester, himself, will 'steal' to Glendower and Mortimer. There is no doubt who is to control the course of the plot:

No further go in this
Than I by letters shall direct your course.

At times, we see him using the rash side of Hotspur's character; sometimes he has problems in controlling the headstrong young man who has developed a personal antipathy to Glendower.

Both the King and Worcester are shrewd politicians and it is one of the interests in the play to observe how they match up to one another, whenever they are in direct conflict. Worcester carefully presents his self-interest as an eagerness to preserve his safety in the face of an oath-breaking monarch. The King clearly sees through this pose:

These things indeed you have articulate,
Proclaimed at market-crosses, read in churches,
To face the garment of rebellion
With some fine colour that may please the eye . . .

Worcester's ability to 'paint' the face of wrong-doing with fine colours is matched by a similar ability in Falstaff.

The machiavellian aspect of Worcester is most obvious when he sees to it that the King's overtures of peace are concealed from Hotspur before the Battle of Shrewsbury. He has perceived the parlousness of the rebel condition, but his only hope of survival must rest in the slim chance of victory – any peace treaty would inevitably spell his doom, for the King could not possibly tolerate his continued existence.

In loading Worcester with most of the odium for the rebellion, Shakespeare manages to preserve Hotspur from the charge of villainy. Thus Hotspur can retain his status and his legendary (if limited) honour and be presented as a fitting rival for the Prince. The honour which thereby accrues to the Prince when he kills Hotspur is relatively untarnished with the taint of wickedness.

Kate

Hotspur's wife, Kate, brings a great deal of charm to the scenes in which she appears. She is obviously, despite her husband's strictures about the inadequacy of her oath-swearing, no wilting flower. When she senses that there is something amiss with Hotspur she taxes him with it directly and playfully threatens his little finger when he refuses to give a satisfactory account of himself. She refuses to sing when requested to do so.

Beneath the banter there is obviously real unease and we sense a pathos in the strains to which an obviously 'good marriage' is put by the demands of insurrection and incipient war.

In showing us glimpses of his private life, Shakespeare enhances our understanding of Hotspur and we see that there is more to him than the public reputation.

Glendower

Glendower, in describing his 'nativity', reveals the poetic side of his character and incidentally arouses the amused contempt of Hostpur, who has no time for such extravagancies. Such a clash of temperaments does not bode well for the rebels. But it would be a mistake to dismiss Glendower as a superstitious fool. His military prowess is evident in that he defeated Mortimer and he is something of a scholar who was 'trained up in the English court', where he learned music, composed songs and wrote poetry. Hardly a Welsh barbarian!

The tavern set

As well as acting as foils (and sometimes butts) for the major characters, the inhabitants of the tavern bring much joy in their own right. The lively, inventive *Poins* provides a fitting 'unfitting' companion for the Prince – he is not a villain and always ready to participate in, and initiate, a practical joke. *Bardolph*, with his red nose and generally grotesque appearance is the source of much visual humour, and 'helps' Falstaff to display his wit. The *Hostess* with her good-natured personality, her idiosyncrasies of speech and basic honesty leads one to reflect that, if she is typical of the lower rungs of society, the England at heart cannot be as rotten as some of the doings of the nobility might lead one to suspect.

These characters, as well as even more 'minor characters' such as *Gadshill* and the *Carriers*, convey the impression that ordinary life in England proceeds much as it always has done, despite the momentous happenings in the main plot. Kings may come and Kings may go but the ordinary folk go about their business.

Structure and style

Structure

The first scene of the play outlines the historical plot and introduces the rivalry between Hal and Hotspur. In the second scene we are introduced to Hal and meet Falstaff – the central figure of the comic plot. As well as the contrast between Hal and Hotspur, it is soon apparent that the theft of a kingdom which the rebels propose is paralleled by the proposed theft at Gad's Hill. The final scene of Act I furthers the rebellion: an open breach occurs between the King and his former allies; and introduces Hotspur whose fiery temperament and sparkling mode of speech contrasts dramatically with the more calculating and measured tones of Hal, which were apparent at the end of the second scene. In addition to the theme of rebellion allied to theft, we are invited also to consider the honour theme and again there is a contrast: Hal lives in dishonour but by the end of the play will have gained it; Hotspur at present has honour and will lose it. Falstaff is clearly without honour.

As the play unfolds so the main plot is paralleled and contrasted with the comic sub-plot. Obviously we are invited to compare the mock interview between Hal and Falstaff, with its counterpart between Hal and his father. In the former Hal rejects his surrogate father, in the latter he embraces his actual father. Hal, of course, is the central figure in the play who unites the main and the sub-plots.

In general the low-life scenes form an ironic contrast with the doings of the mighty. Both Hal and Hotspur flirt with danger, but whereas Hotspur succumbs and allows himself to become embroiled in disorder and rebellion, Hal surmounts danger and disorder to stand eventually foursquare on the side of the angels.

The comic plot arouses and sustains the interest of the audience in the early part of the play, whilst the rebellion is slowly but steadily plotted. The Gad's Hill episode, which we have seen is thematically related to the main disorder theme, is quickly plotted and builds to the climactic moment when Falstaff is 'unmasked'. Strategically situated to keep the audience rapt, the interview-scenes form the nodal part of the middle of the play. We anticipate the scene between Hal and his father because it was part of the 'folk-lore' associated with the story, but the mock interview is a 'surprise', which nonetheless directs our attention forward to Act III Scene 2. Meanwhile, a sense of movement is maintained in the rebel faction by a change of locale to Wales and a dramatic clash between Glendower and Hotspur. Variety of mood is evident, too, with the introduction of Mortimer and his wife, who contrast interestingly with Hotspur and Kate.

Momentum builds in the later part of the play as we look forward to the clash between the Prince and Hotspur. The rebel army arrives at Shrewsbury first, but the suggestion is that Henry's forces are gathering strength and impetus. This is achieved partly by succinct scene endings (Act III Scene 2; Act III Scene 3) and the insertion of a transition scene on 'a road near Coventry.'

There is a time of inaction as King and rebels negotiate before the battle and Hal emerges in chivalric splendour – now clearly a rival for Hotspur's honours. The suggestion of single combat, refused by the King on behalf of Hal, anticipates what is to come in the battle. The battle itself is virtually a series of encounters which build up suspense for the major moment of combat between Hal and Hotspur.

After the Prince's victory, we contemplate its significance, with the 'comic' claim of Falstaff making a sardonic comment on the great event. The play is over, but we leave it on a note of 'things still to be done' which looks forward to the happenings in *Henry IV Part 2*.

Of course, the duel between the two young rivals forms the climax of the play, which 'settles' the hurly-burly which preceded it.

Verse

For the most part Shakespeare adheres to the dramatic convention that the nobility speak in verse, whereas the lower orders speak prose. It seemed fitting to endow the aristocracy with the capacity to think deeper thought and feel finer feelings than the proletariat. There are exceptions to this general rule, as we shall see.

Shakespeare's dramatic blank verse had yet to reach full maturity when he came to write *Henry IV Part 1*, but there are many signs that he was already a master of the medium. A glance at the verse spoken by the King will furnish an example here. At the outset, his words echo his troubled mind (I, 1, 1–4).

The stresses demanded by the blatant alliterations cut across the flow of the iambic pentameter, conveying a sense of awkwardness and strain. This is very different from the commanding flow which is apparent when he addresses the rebels at his next appearance (I, 3, 117–22). This is the King's clipped, business-like style – direct, shorn of imagery and comprising mainly monosyllables: every inch a king. At other times we find that he speaks with similar clarity, and also displays a grasp of his imagery by which the vividness of what he says is enhanced (III, 2, 60–63).

This is very different from the confused, unfinished images of his opening speech. Thus we find that Shakespeare's blank verse enacts the state of mind of the King at the moment at which he speaks and makes the general point that here is a strong man who has his weaknesses.

The finest poetry in the play is spoken by Hotspur. Again several different 'voices' are apparent: most noteworthy are perhaps his rhetorical 'eruptions', when he seems carried away on a stream of high emotion:

Nay, then I cannot blame his cousin king,
That wished him on the barren mountain starve.
But shall it be that you, that set the crown
Upon the head of this forgetful man,
And for his sake wear the detested blot
Of murderous subornation – shall it be
That you a world of curses undergo,
Being the agents, or base second means,
The cords, the ladder, or the hangman rather?
O, pardon me that I descend so low
To show the line and the predicament
Wherein you range under this subtle king!

But Hostpur is also capable of an almost prosaic terseness, combined with an endearing tenderness (II, 3, 90–96).

Here there is also a touch of characteristic wit in the punning on 'cracked crown' (split skulls and counterfeit coins). Hotspur's wit is further evidenced in his conceit on 'honour' (I, 3, 199–206). In this scene we also find the prettily formal description of Mortimer's fight with Glendower 'on the gentle Severn's sedgy bank' – surprising from one who professes to abhor 'mincing poetry'! Such variety of tone which we find from Hotspur is part and parcel of the man – at one moment soldierly, at another romantic, sometimes naive, often impetuous and fiery. He is at his noblest just before battle (V, 3, 92–100).

Beside Hotspur, the verse of Hal seems tame and 'monochromatic'. Some critics think this to be a reflection of the Prince's immaturity – he is a young man as yet uncertain of his true voice. But he is capable of expounding a point with fluidity and emphasis, as he does before his father when he reassures him of his loyalty. But if Hal himself seems rather cool in his verse, it is worth remembering that Vernon's description of him is one of the finest passages in the play (IV, 1, 97–110).

The images proliferate and run into one another creating an impression of godlike strength, vivacity and nobility – a very rich concoction, which threatens to overwhelm the reader. It is a set-piece, which establishes the reformation of the Prince, reminding us in its reference to the 'sun at midsummer' of the promise which Hal made that he would 'imitate the sun', and break through 'the base contagious clouds': a 'glittering' passage.

Prose

The Prince bestrides the 'poetic world' of the nobility and the 'prose world' of the comic sub-plot. When he speaks as a prince it is in verse, when as a member of the tavern society in prose. But the true master of prose is Falstaff, for the command that Shakespeare gives him defines his appeal. The passage about 'honour', in its way, is as vivid as any that is spoken by Hotspur:

> Well, 'tis no matter; honour pricks me on. Yea, but how if honour prick me off when I come on? How then? . . . And so ends my catechism.

Employing a relentless question-and-answer technique (catechism), ironically, Falstaff establishes his lack of faith in honour, which he slowly strips of all its pretensions. Prose is appropriate to the man and to the task. At other times Falstaff's prose is used expansively – to paint a vivid picture, filling in details:

> If I be not ashamed of my soldiers, I am a soused gurnet. I have misused the king's press damnably . . .

and man by man, and moment by moment, Falstaff's scarecrows are summoned to life before us as they march on the road to Coventry. Both passages demonstrate the liveliness of Falstaff's imagination, and the fact that prose is the medium, relates the man more closely to ourselves.

Shakespeare varies the speaking voices of his characters perfectly. There is the affronted Hostess:

> No Sir John, you do not know me, Sir John. I know you, Sir John: you

owe me money, Sir John, and now you pick a quarrel to beguile me of it. I bought you a dozen shirts for your back.

Repetitive, scarcely pausing for breath, she blurts out her indignation. We also meet the humble carriers, complaining inimitably about the inn, using imagery which is at one and the same time, mundane and unforgettably vivid and precise – very different in rhythm from the Hostess:

Second Carrier: Peas and beans are as dank here as a dog. . .

Hotspur, too, occasionally speaks in prose. At the end of Act III Scene 1, when he speaks to Kate, his imagery is all of bourgeois respectability, but the rhythm of his words is staccato, suggesting the underlying restless tension that always surrounds his character. Again, this is contrasted with the Prince, whose prose utterances always seem more measured, even when he has been enjoying himself:

With three or four loggerheads, amongst three or fourscore hogsheads. I have sounded the very base-string of humility. Sirrah, I am sworn brother to a leash of drawers, and can call them all by their christen names, as Tom, Dick and Francis.

Here, and elsewhere, the overall effect is one of control, with the sentences carefully constructed, words precisely used and generally lacking in that feeling of spontaneity, which enlivens the speeches of Falstaff and the other characters we have examined.

It is the glory of Falstaff, that he manages to be in control and convey the impression of spontaneity, and his prose reflects this ability. Never at a loss for words, he is the master of all styles, whether he is parodying the King in the euphuistic, contrived manner of John Lyly, or plucking witty escapes from the thin air ('Should I turn upon the true prince?'), or playing the role of the mock-penitent. In his characterization of Falstaff, Shakespeare demonstrates his genius as a master of dramatic prose.

Imagery

Imagery provides emotional and intellectual illumination on characters, themes and situations in his plays. We shall consider a few examples.

The moon The crest of the Percies was a half-moon and Hotspur by means of various references links himself with the moon: he thinks 'it were an easy leap,/To pluck bright honour from the pale-faced moon'; he feels cheated in the division of England by the winding Trent, which denies him 'a huge half-moon' of land.

Falstaff is associated with the moon, and thus linked with Hotspur – both threatening the order of the state and the royal status of the Prince: 'we that take purses go by the moon'; 'let us be Diana's foresters, gentlemen of the shade, minions of the moon'.

Commerce Hotspur is Hal's 'factor', who must one day pay what is due to his master. The King knows 'when to promise and when to pay'. Falstaff never seems to pay his bills and hates the phrase 'pay back', but he wishes he could buy a 'commodity of good names'. There are also references to the genuineness, or otherwise of coins. The intrusion of commercial values, via this and other similar imagery, presents the nobility in a rather unflattering light. In contrast, however, the Prince fulfils his vow 'to pay the debt he never promised'.

Animals Animal imagery abounds in the play and it is used in a variety of ways. Falstaff is amongst other animals 'roast Manningtree ox', a 'soused gurnet', a 'gib-cat, or a lugged bear'. Some commentators have seen these references as reflecting Falstaff's fundamentally bestial nature. The Prince describes him as 'that bolting-hatch of beastliness'. Throughout the play we find human beings and their characteristics related to a variety of animals – not always derogatorily: the Prince and his companions are like 'eagles', 'youthful goats' and 'estridges'. Shakespeare obviously regarded the animal kingdom as a rich mine of metaphor and he frequently explores our associations with it.

There are many examples in the play of what has been termed 'iterative' (or oft repeated) imagery, by means of which Shakespeare directs our thoughts and feelings about the people and events. But a play is for performance on a stage, and the visual impact of what *happens* is also a sort of imagery. For example, the picture of Falstaff with cushion on head, dagger in hand, and sitting on'A joined stool' is a striking image of disorder. One might also give consideration to the effect on stage of Falstaff stabbing the corpse of Hotspur, and the 'grinning' corpse of Sir Walter Blunt.

General questions

1 Dissolute; undutiful towards his father; cold-hearted and calculating. His sole redeeming feature is his courage.' Comment on this view of Prince Hal.

Suggested notes for essay answer

Dissolute/undutiful?

Indicative of common mistake about Hal's behaviour.

Quote evidence to show Henry IV's opinion from early in play.

Hotspur also misjudges Hal. Quote evidence.

In fact, loose behaviour only a façade.

People mistake the appearance for the reality.

Audience knows the reality after Hal's soliloquy.

Shakespeare reworks the legend of the wild Hal to show that he was not really dissolute;

(a) Distances Hal from real evil.

(b) King, Hotspur and others at given points realize their mistake (note when this happens). Having established that this is just a façade, why does he allow reputation to flourish? He claims he is educating himself. But to justify the pain which he causes his father and the damage done to his reputation and the country, he must be *calculating* that he will achieve a worthwhile purpose.

Calculating?

Undoubtedly – he is playing a part for political motives.

He wishes to become a good king. He is preparing himself.

He may have begun by simply sowing a few youthful wild oats but he has apparently come to see how such behaviour can be turned to positive use.

Disconcerting, because it calls into question much of what he does. Even when he is behaving generously, is it calculated rather than heart-felt?

Consider, in this light:

– the element of 'using people' in his soliloquy;
– the 'Francis episode';
– his treatment of Falstaff;
– Hal's speech over Hotspur's body;
– his willingness to permit Falstaff to take the credit for killing Hotspur;
– his magnanimous setting-free of Douglas, after the battle.
How far do these elements in the play show calculation? Any evidence of cold-heartedness?

We cannot deny the Prince his courage:
– clearly revealed in battle and offer of single combat.
– undaunted by Hotspur's reputation.
– the courage of his convictions: to see the course he has taken through to the end. Also to overcome the temptations represented by Falstaff.

Final comments:
There is no doubt that the Prince acts from lofty motives and he ends the play demonstrably fitted for the role of king, which one day will be his destiny. He has overcome his rival Hotspur; he is united with his father; Falstaff has been all but rejected (final rejection occurs at the end of *Henry IV, Part 2*; he has educated himself about the lower orders of the kingdom. Furthermore, he has revealed a grasp of the nature of kingship: that a king must be a man, a figurehead and a politician.

To achieve his goal, which is ultimately for the good of the nation, there have been sacrifices. The element of political calculation in his behaviour perhaps prevents us from feeling close to the Prince, although we may admire him. He is more subtle than even his father, who does not understand the true motives for Hal's dissoluteness – they have to be explained to him. But the nagging doubt remains that he has knowingly *used* Falstaff, the King, Hotspur and many others.

2 Analyse by means of detailed reference Shakespeare's use of verse and prose.
3 What ideas of kingship, implied or stated, do you find in the play?
4 Write an essay comparing and contrasting Hal and Hotspur.
5 How far do you find Hotspur's reputation justified by his words and actions in the play?

6 'We ought not to like Falstaff, but we all do.' Comment, giving your own opinion of Falstaff.
7 Discuss the theme of honour, as it is revealed in the play.
8 What is the significance of Worcester in the play?
9 Show the inter-relationship between Court and Tavern in the play.
10 What effect is achieved by the scenes which show the domestic life of Hotspur and Kate?
11 In what ways does Hal resemble his father in character in *Henry IV Part 1*?
12 'In Shakespeare's plays there is no such thing as comic relief; his comic scenes and passages are comic reflections of serious issues.' Discuss with reference to *Henry IV Part 1*.
13 'Much of the play's realism results from the masterly creation of minor characters.' Discuss.
14 What evidence is there in this play that Prince Henry will make a good king?
15 'Wer't not for laughing I should pity him.' How far do you share Hal's attitude to Falstaff?
16 What evidence in the play leads us to suppose that the 'madcap Prince' will in the end reform?
17 Show how Shakespeare establishes and develops the rivalry between Hal and Hotspur.
18 Show how Shakespeare's imagery contributes to our understanding of the play.
19 Write a critical appreciation of Hal's epitaph on Hotspur.
20 Analyse in detail the imagery in Vernon's description of Hal and his company in Act IV, Scene 1.
21 Argue for or against the view that in this play Shakespeare is writing propaganda in the cause of law and order.
22 Discuss the structure of the play.
23 In what sense do characters and scenes 'balance' each other in the play?
24 Show how the character of the King develops.
25 Discuss the character of Glendower and contrast him with Hotspur.

Further reading

The Arden Shakespeare: Henry IV Part 1, edited by A. R. Humphreys. An excellent introduction followed by peerless textual glosses (Methuen, 1960, paperback 1966).

Shakespeare's 'Histories': Mirrors of Elizabethan Policy, LILY B. Campbell (Methuen, 1964).

The Elizabethan World Picture, E. M. W. Tillyard (Penguin, 1972).

Shakespeare's History Plays, E. M. W. Tillyard (Chatto, 1980).

Shakespeare from Richard II to Henry V (Hollis and Carter, 1958).

Fortunes of Falstaff, J. D. Wilson (Cambridge University Press, 1979).